# South Africa: The History and Legacy of the Nation from European Colonization to the End of the Apartheid Era

## By Charles River Editors

A picture of Boer militia in 1900

# About Charles River Editors

**Charles River Editors** is a boutique digital publishing company, specializing in bringing history back to life with educational and engaging books on a wide range of topics. Keep up to date with our new and free offerings with this 5 second sign up on our weekly mailing list, and visit Our Kindle Author Page to see other recently published Kindle titles.

We make these books for you and always want to know our readers' opinions, so we encourage you to leave reviews and look forward to publishing new and exciting titles each week.

# Introduction

**A painting of the SS *Cornwall* departing for the Boer War**

## South Africa

"The Boers were hostile toward indigenous African peoples, with whom they fought frequent range wars, and toward the government of the Cape, which was attempting to control Boer movements and commerce. They overtly compared their way of life to that of the Israel patriarchs of the Bible, developing independent patriarchal communities based upon a mobile pastoralist economy. Staunch Calvinists, they saw themselves as the children of God in the wilderness, a Christian elect divinely ordained to rule the land and the backward natives therein. By the end of the 18th century the cultural links between the Boers and their urban counterparts were diminishing, although both groups continued to speak a type of Flemish." – Encyclopaedia Britannica

The Boer War was the defining conflict of South African history and one of the most important conflicts in the history of the British Empire. Naturally, complicated geopolitics underscored it, going back centuries. In fact, the European history of South Africa began with the 1652 arrival of a small Dutch flotilla in Table Bay, at the southern extremity of the African continent, which made landfall with a view to establishing a victualing station to service passing Dutch East India Company (Vereenigde Oost-Indische Compagnie) ships. The Dutch at that point largely dominated the East Indian Trade, and it was their establishment of the settlement of Kaapstad, or Cape Town, that set in motion the lengthy and often turbulent history of South Africa.

For over a century, the Cape remained a Dutch East India Company settlement, and in the interests of limiting expenses, strict parameters were established to avoid the development of a colony. As religious intolerance in Europe drove a steady trickle of outward emigration, however, Dutch settlers began to informally expand beyond the Cape, settling the sparsely inhabited hinterland to the north and east of Cape Town. In doing so, they fell increasingly outside the administrative scope of the Company, and they developed an individualistic worldview, characterized by self-dependence and self-reliance. They were also bonded as a society by a rigorous and literal interpretation of the Old Testament. In their wake, towards the end of the 17th century, followed a wave of French Huguenot immigrants, fleeing a renewal of anti-Protestantism in Europe. They were integrated over the succeeding generations, creating a hybridized language and culture that emerged in due course as the Cape Dutch, The Afrikaner or the Boer.

The Napoleonic Wars radically altered the old, established European power dynamics, and in 1795, the British, now emerging as the globe's naval superpower, assumed control of the Cape as part of the spoils of war. In doing so, they recognized the enormous strategic value of the Cape as global shipping routes were developing and expanding. Possession passed back and forth once or twice, but more or less from that point onwards, the British established their presence at the Cape, which they held until the unification of South Africa in 1910. However, it would only come after several rounds of conflicts.

On June 1, 1948, Daniel Malan arrived in Pretoria by train to take office, and there he was met by a huge crowd of cheering whites. He told the audience, "In the past, we felt like strangers in our own country, but today, South Africa belongs to us once more. For the first time since Union, South Africa is our own. May God grant that it always remain our own." Back in Johannesburg, the leadership of the ANC, including the young attorney Nelson Mandela, listened to these celebratory prognostications in a grim mood. As strangers in their own country, they all understood that the South African liberation struggle would not be won overnight. In fact, the era of apartheid was only just about to formally start.

Although apartheid is typically dated from the late 1940s until its dismantling decades later, segregationist policies had been the norm in South Africa from nearly the moment European explorers sailed to the region and began settling there. Whether it was displacing and fighting indigenous groups like the Khoi and San, or fighting other whites like the Boer, separation between ethnicities was the norm in South Africa for centuries before the election of Malan signaled the true rise of the Afrikaner far right.

The man most associated with dismantling apartheid, of course, is Nelson Mandela. With the official policy of apartheid instituted in 1948 by an all-white government, Mandela was tried for treason between the years of 1956-61 before being acquitted. He participated in the Defiance Campaign of 1952, and oversaw the 1955 Congress of the People, but when the African National Congress was banned in 1960, he proposed a military wing, despite his initial reluctance toward violent resistance, a reluctance which had its roots in original nonviolent protests through the South African Communist Party. The ANC did not openly discourage such an idea, and the Umkhonto we Sizwe was established. Mandela was again arrested in 1962 and tried for attempts to overthrow the government by violence. The sentence was five years of hard labor, but this was increased to a life sentence in 1964, a sentence handed down to seven of his closest colleagues as well.

Mandela would eventually serve 27 years, but his statements made in court received enormous international coverage and acclaim, and his reputation grew during his time in Robben Island Prison of Capetown, the Pollsmoor and Victor Verster Prisons. He was ultimately released in February 1990, in large part as a result of the international campaign generated by his words and the current South African story. Shortly after that, he was elected as the first man of African descent to the presidency of South Africa, which he held from 1994–1999. Most significant was that Mandela was elected from the first multi-factional, multi-racial election ever held in the country, a result of extensive negotiations with then President F.W. Klerk.

*South Africa: The History and Legacy of the Nation from European Colonization to the End of the Apartheid Era* looks at the controversial history of the country, from the initial European explorers to the successful struggle to dismantle apartheid. Along with pictures and a bibliography, you will learn about South Africa like never before.

South Africa: The History and Legacy of the Nation from European Colonization to the End of the Apartheid Era

**The Portuguese**

"One's destination is never a place, but a new way of seeing things." – Henry Miller

Sometime in January 1488, a violent storm blew up off the southern cape of Africa, one of many in a region that would become known for storms. In fact, the storm inspired the cape's first European visitor, the Portuguese mariner Bartolomeu Dias, to name it *Cabo das Tormentas*, or the Cape of Storms. This particular storm, however, caught Dias at a difficult moment, for he was in command of a small flotilla of two caravels, the *São Cristóvão* and the *São Pantaleão*, under commission from King John II of Portugal to round the southern tip of Africa in order to finalize a sea route to the East Indies. With very rudimentary tools of navigation and no charts to work from, where precisely the southern tip of the continent lay remained a matter of educated guesswork.

BARTHOLOMEW DIAZ ON HIS VOYAGE TO THE CAPE.

**An illustration of the two ships**

Portuguese maritime explorers had been gradually probing southwards along the west coast of Africa since the early part of the 15th century, seeding spores of the Portuguese language, religion, and trade interests at numerous points along the way. These journeys were both enterprises in their own right, insofar as trade off the African coast was an end unto itself, as well as an effort to establish Portuguese primacy in the spice trade with India through the discovery of a viable sea route to the east. There was also something of a quasi-religious objective to the undertaking: locating the mythical Kingdom of Prester John, a fabled Christian empire thought to exist somewhere in Africa.

By the time Bartolomeu Dias departed the Portuguese mainland in August 1487, a considerable portion of the route to the Cape had been established, and in practical terms, he was simply joining up the last dots. Speculation on tides and currents tended to suggest that the southern extremity of the African continent was close, but no Europeans knew precisely where it was yet.

In theory, the navigational demands of the voyage were relatively straightforward. It was simply a matter of following the Atlantic coast of Africa until south became east, and then north. The furthest established settlement was the Portuguese fortress of São Jorge da Mina, located on the Gold Coast of what is today Ghana, and perhaps the point furthest known was the desert coast of what is today known as Namibia. There, the two ships could expect to encounter a cold, north-flowing current, the Benguela Current, south of which no expedition had yet passed.

Dias and his crew arrived safely off the coast of what would today be Angola towards the middle of December 1487, reaching the modern Namibian port of Walvis Bay a few weeks later. This was named *Golfo da Conceicão*, and a small cross was erected before the two ships struck out once again for open water.

The next point of landfall was the Namibian port of Lüderitz, named by Dias *Angra dos Ilheus*. Nowhere inland, however, along this parched and arid coast, could the resupply of water or food be obtained, and by then there were serious tensions on board. The two ships were entering latitudes never before challenged, and the cold current coming up from the Antarctic provoked jitters among men, some of whom still believed the world was flat.

Then, abruptly, the storm hit, and the fleet was pushed far out into the Atlantic, and all that Dias could know for certain was that the ships lay somewhere west and south of their last known position. How far south was impossible to know, as navigational technology was crude and the ships were by then well beyond sight of land. An easterly course would end up carrying them in the direction of the mainland, but if by chance they had drifted to a latitude below the southern tip of Africa, they would have no idea when they sailed past it.

This was a very fundamental conundrum, and it was completely bewildering to sailors of that era. Falling back on instinct, Dias set a course due east and hoped for the best. A day passed, and then another one, but still all that could be seen from the crow's nest of the *São Cristóvão* was open ocean. Two options were now open to him – either hold firm and continue east, at the risk of missing their objective altogether (and sailing blindly into the Indian Ocean), or turn north at the risk of returning back in the direction from which they had come.

Dias' instincts told him to hold steady on an easterly course, but under pressure from his crew he reluctantly agreed to turn northeast, and this quickly proved to be a fateful decision. The expedition had indeed overshot the southern cape, and when, after sailing for 30 days without sight of land, land was eventually sighted, it turned out to be modern-day Mossel Bay in South Africa, some 150 miles east of the Cape. They named this region *Aguada de São Brás*. The date was February 4, 1488, and although Bartolomeu Dias would proceed only a short distance further east along the coast than this, it was more or less on that date that he realized the way now lay open to India.

Somewhat inadvertently, Dias and his crew had accomplished one of the most crucial feats of navigation, and in many respects it was the crowning achievement of a process begun at the dawn of the 15th century under the patronage of one of the great geniuses and innovators of the age. The name "Henry the Navigator" has become intimately associated with the mythology and history of the Age of Exploration, and at the very least it was he who set in motion the great age of Portuguese exploration. Known in his day as Prince Henry, or *Infante Henrique*, he was the son of King John I of Portugal, known best for his preservation of Portuguese sovereignty and the founding of the Aviz Dynasty, of which Henry was a member.

**Henry the Navigator**

**King John I of Portugal**

The reign of John I coincided more or less with the expulsion of the Moors from Portugal, but pockets of Muslim resistance remained in Spain and bitter fighting continued for a long time. When Henry was about 16, John decided to launch a campaign against the North African mainland, seizing the crucial port of Ceuta, a Muslim stronghold located immediately across the Straits of Gibraltar. This was a great and comprehensive military victory, attributable in many respects to the young Henry's planning. That campaign established him at an early age in the minds of his people as a great military and naval commander.

**A depiction of Prince Henry the Navigator at Ceuta**

Henry was born in 1394, on the cusp of monumental changes in Europe and the world, and as a child he certainly dreamed of great military conquests and fame as a military leader. In the aftermath of Ceuta, however, and as riches from the African continent began arriving in Lisbon, his mind began to turn to a more daring conquest of Africa by means of exploration and trade. It was this fascination that set in motion the series of voyages that would culminate in Bartolomeu Dias' discovery of the Cape of Storms.

Henry was one of three brothers, and he was not originally in line for the throne. He thus remained a prince, and until the age of 26 he was actively involved in the wars and campaigns of his father, winning his spurs in numerous campaigns and battles. A major change came in 1420 when he was placed in charge as administrator general of the Holy Order of Christ, the successor of the Knights Templar in Portugal. From then on, at least according to popular history, his twin preoccupations became religion and exploration.

Although Henry never set sail on a single expedition himself, it was his funding and patronage (not to mention the development of appropriate ships and navigational techniques) that drove Portugal's momentum. By then, the Portuguese had ventured as far south along the African coast as the Canary Islands, but Henry, having personally seen the goods carried north by caravan across the Sahara Desert, was aware that slaves and gold were to be found in large quantities somewhere further to the south, and he was anxious to circumvent the Muslim trade networks of North Africa by locating the source. How far south beyond the desert the continent of Africa extended was anyone's guess, but he intended to find out.

One of the most important discoveries was the phenomenon known as the *Volta do mar*, or the "turn of the sea," which in practical terms is a rotating system of winds and currents in the mid-Atlantic that allowed an outward journey via the Canary Islands and a return journey via the Azores. It This facilitated the triangulated three-point traffic of the Atlantic slave trade, allowing for a journey along the coast to African slave ports, the trans-Atlantic "Middle Passage," and a journey directly home from the Caribbean.

**A map of the Middle Passage**

The Azores, Madeira and the Canaries marked the main points of the first journeys out, with Cape Bojador in modern Western Sahara the most southerly known point on the West African coast. In 1434, Cape Bojador was passed by Gil Eanes, one of Henry's commanders, and compatriots Nuno Tristão and Antão Gonçalves reached Cape Blanco off the coast of modern Mauritania in 1441. In 1443, a fort was constructed on the Bay of Arguin, also in Mauritania, which set the stage for the first probing movement south of the Sahara Desert. Soon the mouth of the Senegal River was reached, at which point Henry could claim to have successfully circumnavigated the Muslim trade networks of North Africa. Before long, gold and slaves began to arrive in Portugal, at which point most of Henry's critics were silenced.

Bartolomeu Dias did not press on much further into the Indian Ocean than the site of his landing. Naturally, he returned in haste to Lisbon, arriving in December 1488 after an absence of 16 months and 17 days. The way to India had been established, and the next to appear in the waters of the southern Indian Ocean was the more famous Portuguese mariner Vasco da Gama. It was da Gama who would round what was now renamed *Cabo da Boa Esperança*, or the Cape of Good Hope, in 1497, and he would reach India in May 1498.

## A depiction of da Gama reaching India

**A map of da Gama's routes**

Vasco da Gama's route from the Cape to India was quite straightforward. Annually alternating trade winds carried him up the East African coast, and in some respects, he was back in known waters. The ancient trade route between India and Europe followed the coast of Arabia into the Red Sea, and by land across the Isthmus of Suez. This linked the shipping fleets of the Mediterranean with those of the Red Sea, and it established subsequent links and connections along the coast of the Arabian Peninsula and the Persian Gulf to ports in Gujarat and as far south as the coast of Goa. By knowing that he was indeed on the coast of East Africa, it was easy for da Gama to simply sail north along the coast, pausing at various points until crossing the Gulf of Aden. There he contacted Arab and Indian merchants who directed him east to the coast of India.

As was true of all the European trading powers that would eventually follow in the footsteps of these early Portuguese explorers, it was not Portuguese imperial policy to try to seize or control territory on the mainland for its own sake. Instead, depots and forts were established for the sole purpose of conducting trade with the existing powers of the coast and the interior. These facilities inevitably grew into settlements as missionaries arrived and colonists assimilated, married locals, and established roots. The same was true for the Danes, the French, the Dutch and British, who all founded similar settlements as they joined the slave trade and lay the groundwork for future spheres of influence. Conditions in the interior were simply too hostile to contemplate colonization, and it would be several more centuries before wider exploration and exploitation of Africa's interior was even attempted.

Further south, as Portuguese exploration continued, their parties encountered an increasingly arid coastline and a cold, northward moving current. Apart from one or two landings and a few monuments erected, no attempt was made to establish any kind of permanent settlement here. In fact, despite regularly visiting the peninsula, the green and splendid Cape of Good Hope was also left unsettled by the Portuguese. This was mainly because the elusive natives were too wild and few in numbers to justify the hunt, and there was no one on shore willing or able to trade anything that was of interest to the Portuguese. The future would demonstrate that this was a blunder, because in 1652 the Dutch would assume control of the region, representing a lost opportunity for the Portuguese. The modern provincial structure of South Africa includes the province of Natal, marked by the Portuguese on the developing map of Africa, and named after the Christmas Day when it was first sighted. Once again, however, it was never permanently settled.

The Dutch were more than a century behind the Portuguese in making landfall in southern Africa, which gave the Portuguese centuries of unrestricted access before other European colonizing powers began to appear on the scene. The coast of West Africa, thanks to powerful kings and rampant malaria, did not invite deeper exploration, but East Africa certainly did. The Arabs had already established widespread and comprehensive trade networks throughout the region, and all that was required now was for the Portuguese to force the Arabs out and take over all of that themselves. Before long, the Portuguese had effectively taken over all the key Swahili ports and settlements along the coast as far north as Mogadishu, and in 1507 they entered the port of Muscat on the Arabian Peninsula, the capital of the Omani Sultanate, which they held for 143 years.

The Portuguese tended thereafter to confine themselves to the coast and the lower reaches of the Zambezi, conducting trade expeditions into the interior until, by the late 17th century, the tribes of the Central Plateau had ceased to exist as a dynasty. Gold reserves were depleted, and shortly after that the Portuguese lost interest in the region, focusing their efforts instead on the trade arteries of the Zambezi and the Limpopo, and as well as the rapidly growing East African slave trade.

**The Arrival of the Dutch**

To understand what led to the Dutch's sudden prominence, one must travel back to 1568. Before the mid-1500s, the territories known as Belgium and Holland today were composed of 17 lowland provinces belonging to Burgundy. These lands came under the control of Charles V, King of Spain and Holy Roman Emperor, in 1506. In 1568, his son, Philip II, intervened in said territories once more to quell the movement of the Protestant Reformation, but disgruntled dwellers in the 5 northern provinces did not take kindly to this and revolted against the king. 11 years later, 7 of the provinces officially declared their independence with the Union of Utrecht. From then on, they dubbed themselves the United Provinces. Just 6 years later, the Siege of Antwerp of 1585 drew a dashed line between Northern and Southern Netherlands, formally dividing the regions.

**Charles V**

**Philip II**

Before the siege, the city of Antwerp was the leading center of commerce in all of Europe. Antwerp welcomed Catholic and Protestant merchants alike, and it was this unbiased attitude that propelled them to the top of the ladder. Merchants from Germany, England, and the new United Provinces all flocked to Antwerp to trade an assortment of goods, including grains, Baltic timber, and exquisite Dutch textiles. One of the commodities Dutch merchants readily accepted was Iberian salt, which was used in preserving herring and other Dutch delicacies.

The decision made by Alexander Farnese, the Duke of Parma, to invade Antwerp came with lasting consequences. Going against the tradition of ruling Catholic powers of the time, Farnese allowed Protestants to evacuate the city peacefully. At the same time, Philip II, Farnese's uncle, imposed a ban on trade against the United Provinces and confiscated all trading ships from the ports of Spain and Portugal. The king had unwittingly created a population of roaming Antwerp Protestants, the majority of which were skilled craftsmen, seamen, and wealthy merchants. Backed by years and experience of international trade, they would soon take the industry by storm.

**Farnese**

Most Protestant refugees made their new homes in the city of Amsterdam. The population in the capital of Holland, then an obscure trading port, ballooned from 30,000 residents to 105,000. The multicultural community of Amsterdam had quickly become one of the most highly populated cities in all of Europe.

From then on marked a glowing period of religious, scientific, technological, and artistic advancements in Holland. The world was introduced to the creative genius of Rembrandt and Pieter Hooft, as well as the likes of Christiaan Huygens, who invented the pendulum clock. In the late 16th century, Holland decided that they, too, wanted in on the spice trade.

In 1591, the Portuguese established a syndicate between German, Italian and Spanish firms, utilizing Hamburg as its central port. This syndicate essentially excluded the Dutch from nautical trade. Infuriated Dutch merchants vowed to find a way into the industry themselves, beginning with their observations as the Portuguese trading system fell apart. To start off, the syndicate could not match the increasing demands of certain commodities, especially pepper, and each time the syndicate failed to meet the supply quota for pepper, the spice saw a dramatic increase in prices. The Dutch finally found their way in when a couple of traveling merchants, Cornelius de Houtman and Jan Huyghen van Linschoten, allegedly gained access to confidential Portuguese trade routes and learned their business practices.

**A portrait of van Linschoten**

In 1594, Reiner Pauw, Jean Corel, and Dirk van Os, along with a small group of merchants hailing from Antwerp and Amsterdam, established a syndicate of their own. They called their new company the "Compagnie van Verre" – the Company of Far Lands. The next year, the CFL sent 249 sailors, spread over 4 ships, to India on a quest for spices and other blue-chip items.

After 3 years of rough seas and the mini-battles that ensued abroad, only 89 Dutch crewmen made their way back to Holland. On top of their obvious lack of planning and shoddy organizational skills, the ships returned with only a single cargo of pepper, and little to no other spices or valuable goods. Nevertheless, even with the seemingly unimpressive haul, merchants were still able to make a tidy profit.

The phenomenon excited other wealthy Dutch merchants, who found a fresh opportunity and pounced on it. That same year, in 1597, Vincent van Bronkhorst, Cornelius van Campen, and another band of Dutch merchants formed a company of their own. They called it the "Nieuwe Compagnie te Amsterdam (New Company of Amsterdam)." By 1599, 6 new companies from Rotterdam, Delft, and Zeeland, all motivated by the same agenda, had come to fruition.

Among these companies was one founded by a reputable merchant, Isaac Le Maire. Le Maire joined forces with merchants from different Dutch cities, including Louis de la Beeque and Jacques de Velaer, and founded the Nieuwe Brabantse Compagnie. Later that year, Amsterdam's burgomasters (mayor-like officials) gifted the NBC a charter for trade with China. The following year, NBC was permitted to partner up with Expert Compagnie, forming the newly united Verinigde Compagnie te Amsterdam (the United Amsterdam Company). 8 massive ships fit to fight the most passionate of waters were added to the merged company's assets, which were to be commanded by Captain Jacob van Neck.

Qui secta lustravit Batavis incognita Nautis,
et non visa priùs per Gallos, atque Britannos,
ac Lusitanos Indorum nomine claros,
Christicolasvè alios, sulcantes æquora velis,
sic sua Iacobus Lemarius ora serebat.

**Le Maire**

**Van Neck**

In late 1600, van Neck's ships produced results that put a sparkling grin on the faces of Dutch merchants everywhere. His successful voyage became the first to touch bases with the "Spice Islands" of Maluku. This eliminated the need for Javanese middlemen, and in turn, Dutch merchants raked in a 400% profit. It was then that the Dutch knew they were truly in business.

At that point, it was high time for retaliation. In the spirit of the Portuguese syndicate, the Dutch companies realized that unity would be the key to driving the Portuguese out of the spice industry. In the last weeks of 1600, the Dutch collaborated with Muslim merchants on the Ambon Island of Indonesia. Their agreement entailed that the Dutch be granted exclusive rights to the purchasing of all spices on the island.

Traditionally, European maritime companies operated under one similar and increasingly dated system. Unlike modern corporations today, an entire company would be established for the purpose of a single round trip voyage to the East Indies. Once what was left of the ships returned, the company disintegrated. The defunct company then distributed profits between shareholders, and proceeded to either sell or auction off their inventory and equipment. Conversely, the new Dutch establishments set out to change the antiquated system, breathing "semi-permanent life" into their companies. While most companies were formed to take on just one voyage, the Dutch were granted a single charter that allowed them to oversee a series of them. This meant that rather than having a constant rotation of control, the same set of directors and board members were kept on staff throughout the voyages. Finally, when the voyages were deemed complete, the same directors would take the profit and capital from the now buried companies to start a brand new one.

In 1601, the Dutch were on a mission to quench their spice cravings. 6 of these companies released 65 ships on 14 voyages to the Cape of Good Hope, the rocky border in the Cape Peninsula of South Africa. The scramble for spices took a definitive toll on the nation's trade. While bidding prices in Indonesia soared, merchants in Amsterdam were forced to lower their prices as local competition began to heat up.

Profits were at an all-time low. The Dutch government, which felt its power dwindling, knew the problem had to be remedied, and fast. If the Dutch did not act now, the swelling unified powers of Portugal and Spain would push them out of the industry altogether, rendering all their accomplishments thus far completely useless. Meanwhile, a more ominous threat loomed over the Dutch market, as the English were already one step ahead of them. Just a year before, English seafaring companies combined their powers in one of the world's earliest monopoly enterprises: the British East India Company.

On March 20, 1602, the Dutch followed by example, marking another page in history. The 6 rival companies – the United Amsterdam Company, the Veerse Compagnie, the Verenigde Zeeuwse Compagnie, the Magellaanse Rotterdamse Compagnie, the Moucheron van der Hagen & Compagnie, the Een andere Rotterdamse Compagnie, and the Delftse Vennooteschappe Compagnie – combined their powers into a single entity. The new "mega-merger" of a corporation became known as Vereenigde Oostindische Compagnie – formally referred to as the United Dutch Chartered East India Company. Traders from the nearby cities of Enkhuizen and Hoorn were also invited to the trade of the newly-formed cartel, now known today as the Dutch East India Company.

With blessings from the Dutch government and a starting capital of approximately 6,440,200 guilders (roughly $644 million in USD today), the VOC could now reign as a monopoly over all Asian trade. The charter bestowed upon the company the right to build and maintain armies, erect forts overseas, and the power to handle treaties with Asian rulers however they saw fit. This charter, which would be valid for 21 years, also suggested that board members perform a routine audit every 10 years.

It was under the purview of the Dutch East India Company that a small flotilla of trading vessels arrived on the southern peninsula of the African continent in 1652. The expedition was led by Company factor Jan van Riebeeck, and its objective was to establish a victualling station for passing ships of the Company. A settlement was founded and before long, the city of Cape Town, in the shadow of the famous Table Mountain, began to take root.

**Jan van Riebeeck**

## Indigenous Peoples

One of the first things that Riebeeck did was establish a boundary separating the Company compound from the surrounding native communities. He did this by planting a bitter almond hedge around the settlement, beyond which no employee of the Company was authorized to settle. In part, the hedge was intended to establish and limit the responsibility of the Company, but also to prevent any undue interference with native communities and limit the interactions of an almost exclusively male Dutch community with local native women. It would, however, also establish a fundamental doctrine of separation in the new colony, defining and symbolizing South Africa as a nation built on a foundation of segregation.

Beyond the almond hedge and in the extensive hinterland of the *Kaap de Goede Hoop*, or the Cape of Good Hope, there did indeed reside an indigenous society. These were known by the Dutch as "Hottentot," an onomatopoeic term referencing the phonetic click that characterized their language. The word "Hottentot" is still occasionally used today, but it has become rather discredited. Instead, the same society is more accurately known as "Khoisan," and in southern Africa, then as now, it defines two distinct races: the San, or Bushmen, and the Khoi, or Khoikhoi.

The Khoisan are an ancient people representing the earliest human inhabitants of the region, with an archaeological record dating back at least 100,000 years before the first arrival of the Europeans. Beyond that, the archaeological record is illuminated by only a few pinpricks of discovery here and there that place some of the earliest human ancestors in South Africa. These are classified as *australopithecines*, literally "southern apes." The first major discovery of australopithecine remains in South Africa was made in 1924 by Witwatersrand University Professor Raymond Dart in a cave system known as Taung, located in what is today the North-West province of South Africa. Similar remains have also been discovered in a series of limestone caves at Sterkfontein, Swartkrans, and Kromdraai, all now collectively classified as a UNESCO World Heritage Site. This particular region of South Africa, located to the northwest of Pretoria, is now rather aptly known as the "Cradle of Humankind."

It was the Khoisan who were living around Table Bay when van Riebeeck and his party landed on the beach, and it was in that vicinity that the two groups first encountered one another. The indigenous people maintained a nomadic hunter-gatherers society, and the enormous social and political ramifications that followed van Riebeeck's arrival on the shores of the Cape eventually displaced them or caused them to be eradicated. Most now survive only in the arid west of the subcontinent, where they remain relatively primitive and nomadic, for the most part eschewing contact with modern societies. Their social and political organization extended no further than small family groups, and they spoke what must have seemed a bizarre and incomprehensible language. Occupying a wide range of the southern continent, their numbers were small and their impact on the land was minimal.

Perhaps the most interesting aspect of San culture was the artistic legacy they left in the form of parietal art in cave sites all over southern Africa. Most of these are minor, but in many places, large, multi-generational compositions survive, presenting an opus of beautifully rendered compositions of animals and human hunters. In what is now Zimbabwe, horses and riders are portrayed, documenting the arrival of whites.

The Khoikhoi resembled the San – small in stature, almond-eyed, and with signature peppercorn hair – but they were pastoral in habit, and although also nomadic, their lifestyles tended to be more material. In the same vein, their social and political order seemed more established. They nonetheless existed as a nomadic people, thinly dispersed and limited to family or clan groups. The San did not represent a particular presence in the Cape in the 17th century, but the Khoikhoi had long been established on the well-watered pasture lands of the Cape, and it was they who confronted the first European arrivals. The first record of contact with the natives was documented by early Portuguese mariners, who stopped over briefly at the Cape as they explored the southern reaches of the continent. They did not settle the Cape, however, instead starting settlements in the future Mozambique and elsewhere up the coast as they charted the first successful sea passage from Europe to India.

Initially, the Dutch established virtually no contact with the Khoisan, relying instead on imported slaves from elsewhere in Africa and from various parts to the east for labor. They found the natives simply too primitive to exploit and too few in number to represent either a threat or a resource. The story is often told of Cape Colony Governor Simon van der Stel adopting a Khoisan child, educating him, and sending him overseas. Upon his return, the boy, now an adult, promptly abandoned his European clothes and returned to his own people, provoking a philosophical debate on the wisdom and viability of assimilation.

**Simon van der Stel**

In general, the only impact that the Dutch arrival had on the Khoi and San was to introduce non-native diseases to which both groups proved extremely vulnerable, ensuring that their numbers, already small, were reduced even further. At the same time, the San, as a hunter-gatherer society and with an elemental sense of nature and property, found European herds difficult to resist, and stock theft was endemic. This eventually resulted in their systematic eradication by way of bounties.

Initially, very little land was taken, and the Khoikhoi families in occupation of the peninsula simply moved away. As the settlement of the Cape developed, the lack of white women tended to see an inevitable incidence of sexual exploitation of the Khoisan women, with the result that a sub-culture referred to in South Africa as "colored" began to develop. Today, that community is broadly divided by rural and urban origins. Rural members of the group derive typically from the interaction of European and "Hottentot," while urban members had a much more diverse genetic lineage with the influence of white and Khoisan as well as Indian, Arab, and the many different ethnicities of slaves that were present in the Cape at that time. The urban community is today distinct and established from whites, and it has rich and vibrant social traditions that developed over centuries . The rural community, on the other hand, occupied a niche as agricultural laborers, and in many places they continue to do those jobs. Their genetic proximity to the Khoisan is evident in their appearance, so much so that they represent the only surviving manifestation of the original Khoikhoi population today.

The Dutch character of the European population was both diluted and enriched somewhat toward the end of the 17th century. After about 40 years of settlement, a wave of French Huguenots fleeing religious persecution in Europe sought refuge among an isolated society of Dutch Calvinists celebrating a Protestant tradition. These two highly accomplished European cultures mingled in that isolation, and although they remained substantively European, they absorbed the cultural and genetic influences of their Asian and Micronesian slaves, establishing the bedrock of the unique "Cape Dutch" culture and society of the modern Cape.

As the Cape developed into a permanent, diverse, Dutch and French-speaking settlement, the original Company decree that no person shall settle beyond the bitter almond hedge became increasingly moot. It was inevitable after a while that Europeans would begin to extend outward from Cape Town, pressing north, west, and especially east along the fertile and well-watered coastal hinterland. As a result, there evolved a rugged breed of frontier pastoralists who assumed the name of *Boere*, or farmer, and sometimes *Trekboere*, or migrating farmer.

As generations of Boer steadily expanded their settlements eastward, separating from their metropolitan cousins in Cape Town, they began to hybridize. Adopting a strict, Calvinist religious credo, they relied on a literal interpretation of the Old Testament, by which they began to regard themselves as a chosen people. They also considered land upon which they migrated a promised land and viewed the native tribes as Canaanites, who were to be persecuted and banished.

This process of Boer expansion continued until the 1770s, at which point some of them reached the west bank of the Great Fish River in what is today the Eastern Cape. There, for the first time, they encountered the Bantu, and the peaceful migration of both groups was abruptly interrupted.

The word *Bantu*, in anthropological terms, broadly defines the indigenous races of Africa making up the bulk of its modern population. The word is a variant of the Nguni term *abaNtu*, meaning "people" or "the people" as an expression of humanness, humanity, or simply being human. It was first used in this context by German linguist Wilhelm Bleek in his 1862 study *A Comparative Grammar of South African Languages*, from where it has since entered the language of African anthropological study.

The Bantu were the subject of a vast migration over many centuries that saw the Congoid establish its dominance over the virtual entirety of sub-Saharan Africa. The "Bantu Migration," or the "Bantu Expansion," exists today as a contested hypothesis rather than an established historical fact. The currently accepted theory places the origins of the Bantu race in the broad region of the Niger Delta. Their outward migration was driven primarily by the development of agriculture and ironwork, and the enhanced opportunities that the advances presented. South and eastward migration brought about the gradual displacement of older Neolithic populations such as the San who were well established south of the equator. Sometime around the beginning of the 2nd millennium CE, the Bantu Expansion reached and then crossed the Limpopo River, entering the region.

The Bantu Migration, when it reached South Africa, was split by the central highlands of the Drakensberg mountain range. One part migrated east onto the coastal littoral of Natal, and the other veered west, occupying the South African Highveld.[1] The former became the Nguni and the latter the Basutho, or Basutho-Tswana, who occupied the Highveld and the north and northwestern provinces of modern South Africa. The commencement of Bantu settlement in South Africa is tentatively dated at about 500 CE.

In the meanwhile, the Nguni streamed down onto the coastal plain, evolving eventually into the major South African language groups of the Zulu and Xhosa. Over the course of successive decades, they continued their slow migration south, progressively settling the verdant and fertile country of Natal. By the end of the 18th century, however, the southern extent of Xhosa settlement, when it reached the Great Fish River, encountered the northern and eastern extent of Boer expansion, and both migrations were abruptly halted.

At this point, there is a debate over exactly what happened. White South African history asserts

---

[1] Natal was name given to the east coast of South Africa by the Portuguese, who observed it on Christmas day, and Highveld is a term that applies to the land lying above 5,000ft in north-central South Africa.

that the Bantu were absent from the Cape at the beginning of Dutch occupation, which certainly was true. The region was populated by the Khoisan, and the first contact with the Bantu took place as described above. This fact was used throughout the apartheid period as the basis of a claim of prior occupation, which, under the circumstances, is hard to dispute. As a facet of history, however, this tends to sit uncomfortably with black history, and as a historical concept, it is generally rejected.

Regardless, the encounter between the black Bantu and white Boer triggered the first of what came to be known as the "Kaffir Wars" or "Frontier Wars," a conflict that ebbed and flared for a century or more until the pacification and subjugation of blacks in South Africa was completed around the end of the 19th century.[2]

In the past, historians have been fond of illustrating this clash of societies as the breaking of a wave. The Bantu Migration flowed south from its origins in West Africa, was channeled by the Great Rift Valley, and eventually brought the Bantu to the southern subcontinent. There, the movement was divided by the Drakensberg, quickening its pace down the coastal region until it broke against a seawall of white occupation. A backwash, of course, was inevitable, and in the turbulence that followed, an age of peaceful migration transmuted into an age of militancy and war.

The Frontier Wars were, of course, part of this phenomenon, but even greater permutations took place within black society itself. For the very first time, competition for space and resources introduced the need for confederation, so tribes and clans coalesced into larger and more powerful entities to compete with and protect against others doing the same. There were other external influences to consider as well. For example, in Delagoa Bay on the east coast, the Portuguese developed a trading relationship with the tribes of the interior, introducing the medium of exchangeable wealth and bringing with it some inevitable tensions and competition. A Portuguese sailor who was shipwrecked off the Natal coast and subsequently traveled through the region to Delagoa Bay (today the southeast coast of Mozambique) wrote, "These people are herdsmen and cultivators . . . their main crop is millet which they grind between two stones in wooden mortars to make flour. From this they make cakes [and] of the same grain make beer . . . they drink with great gusto. Their cattle are numerous, fat, tasty and large, the pastures being very fertile. Their wealth consists mainly in their huge number of dehorned cows."[3]  About a century later, a Dutch sailor also shipwrecked off Natal reported, "The country is exceedingly fertile, and incredibly populous, and full of cattle, whence it is that lions and other ravenous animals are not apt to attack men as they find enough tame cattle to devour."[4]

Thus, by the end of the 18th century, the ingredients for a great conflagration were in place,

---

[2] The word 'Kaffir' his highly pejorative in modern South Africa, although it's original usage as a general term for black was quite general. It is derived form the Arabic term 'kafir', meaning infidel, or heretic, and was used in reference to black slaves who non-Muslim.

[3]  Reader, John. *Africa: A Biography of the Continent*. Page 442.

[4]  Reader, John. *Africa: A Biography of the Continent*. Page 442—443.

requiring only a spark to set it off. That spark proved, in the end, to be the birth in 1787 of an illegitimate child to the daughter of a noble family and the son of a minor chieftain of the Zulu clan. The mother's name was Nandi, the father was Senzangakhona, and the child was Shaka.

The name Shaka resonates with enormous power and authority throughout modern South African history, but the boy in question began his life as a fugitive, as his mother was an outcast who was reviled for his illegitimate birth. Historians have also speculated that Shaka was perhaps homosexual or sexually impotent, for which he compensated in the context of his times through a ruthless propensity for violence.

Toward the end of the 18th century, the region of Natal was dominated by two major groups, the Mthethwa and Ndwandwe, ruled respectively by two powerful kings, Dingiswayo and Zwide. Both comprised of numerous minor tribes and clans and were at almost perpetual war with one another. The Zulu clan belonged to the Mthethwa confederation, and in common with all initiated boys, Shaka was eventually inducted into the Mthethwa army, a life that he took to like a duck to water. Through a combination of extreme physicality, intelligence, and creativity, he quickly rose through the ranks, and no less quickly in the estimations of Dingiswayo. When his father, Senzangakhona, died in 1816, the throne of the Zulu was passed down to his son and heir Sigujana, Shaka's legitimate half-brother. Sigujana's reign, however, would prove to be short. With Dingiswayo's help, Shaka marched on the royal kraal of the Zulu, killed Sigujana, and assumed the throne himself.

Although it was perhaps an insignificant coup in the grand scheme of things, especially with various imperial powers establishing global empires, this was a pivotal moment in South African history. The Zulu had previously been an inconsequential clan with just a small army, but Shaka immediately set about fashioning his minor tribe into a formidable fighting force, implementing a relentless regime of discipline and introducing new weapons and tactics. He exchanged the traditional javelin for a short stabbing spear known as the *Iklwa*, a name that mimicked the sound of the blade as it was withdrawn from the body. He also introduced the shock tactics of hand-to-hand combat that had previously never been used. With his initial force of some 600 men, he then began subjugating smaller, regional clans and tribes, quickly building his own proto-confederacy.

Although he observed Shaka's actions closely, Dingiswayo allowed this to take place, content that Shaka would form a buffer between the Mthethwa and the Ndwandwe. At the same time, Shaka was careful to stay on the right side of Dingiswayo, dedicating his conquests and all of his booty to the Paramount.

In 1817, however, Dingiswayo was killed during a campaign against the Ndwandwe, and Shaka seized the opportunity to rally the Mthethwa army under his command. After comprehensively defeating Zwide and the Ndwandwe, he assumed the role of Paramount himself.

This began the meteoric rise of the Zulu nation. Shaka maintained the same basic terms of confederacy, ruling as a paramount chief over numerous allied and subject tribes and clans, each of which contributed men to the regimental structure of the Zulu army and enjoyed the protection of the confederation. Shaka then embarked on a program of aggressive expansion in all directions, spearheaded by a military machine the like of which had never been seen before. Within a few years, Shaka's Zulu ruled an empire covering the entire region of Natal north of Tugela River, known thereafter as Zululand.

**A 19ᵗʰ century European depiction of Shaka holding an *assegai* and large shield**

These had a major regional effect, and today it is a phenomenon known as the *Mfecane*, or the "Scattering." As the Zulu rapidly and violently expanded, tribes and clans were displaced, creating a knock-on effect that saw militant and aggressive groups such as the amaNdebele, under the despotic king Mzilikazi, bringing warfare and destruction in every direction they traveled. As one group was displaced, it moved on to displace another, creating a wave of destruction across the entire region. This pattern continued until the 1840s, and those three decades of violence, depopulation, and famine brought about an astronomical loss of life.

The Mfecane outlived Shaka, who was assassinated by his half-brother Dingane in 1828. By then, Shaka had by all accounts, descended into a state of sociopathic violence and paranoia, turning on his own people in an orgy of fratricidal killing that only ended with his death. The Zulu nation never quite replicated the glorious era of Shaka, but under the leadership of Dingane and subsequent kings, it remained a formidable military nation that would collide with white settlers as they gradually advanced into the African interior.

**19th century European illustration depicting Dingane in civilian and military attire**

**19<sup>th</sup> century European illustration of a Zulu warrior**

## The Great Trek

As the Napoleonic Wars played out in Europe, the Dutch allied with the French, which proved to be a mistake when Napoleon met his Waterloo in 1815. William V, Prince of Orange, had sought asylum in England years earlier, and in 1795 he had ordered the Batavian governor of Cape Town to hand over the administration of the colony to the British. This was resisted, and a brief skirmish was fought to enforce it, but more or less, from that moment on, the Cape was established as a British overseas territory. In an age of European imperial expansion, the southern tip of Africa was simply too important a strategic location for the British Royal Navy not to control it.

The British had many profound effects, but perhaps the greatest was the impact that it had on the Frontier Wars and on the lives and liberty of the Boer. With regard to the former, British command and a force of arms turned the tide of the conflict very much against the Xhosa. A consequence of the latter was that the British administration curbed the independent lifestyles of the Boer, brought them under the rule of British law, and imposed abolition on what was then a slave-owning society.

The takeover of the Cape by the British was generally unpopular among the Dutch, but the urban and settler elites tended to accept it, and they generally benefited. They did not like the British, of course, but they were pragmatic about the material effects. The Boer, on the other hand, who were mostly bucolic and rural, were outraged and resisted the British bitterly. This established deep mutual antipathy between the Boers and Britain that would prove so influential on South African history deep into the 20th century.

**A Boer family in the 1880s**

The net result of this was a decision taken in the early 1830s by a radical fringe of Boer to leave the Cape region altogether, in an organized exodus known as the Great Trek. This carried waves of migrating Boer, known as Voortrekkers, or Forward-movers, north into the unsettled interior of the subcontinent. Beyond the Vaal River, and east into the future Natal, the migrating Boer came up against two powerful, independent native kingdoms, the Zulu and the amaNdebele. Several dramatic engagements took place that saw isolated Boer parties attacked by significant legions of disciplined native infantry, but since the Boer were armed with traditional weapons and used cannonades and musketry against their opponents' mounted assaults, these tribes were ultimately defeated. Such improbable victories as these, against such phenomenal odds, established the bedrock of Boer mythology and served to confirm to a pious people that this was indeed a land promised to them by God.

Three Boer republics were thereafter founded. These were the Orange Free State (Oranje-Vrijstaat), the Transvaal, or Zuid-Afrikaansche Republiek (ZAR), and the Republic of Natalia. The first two were landlocked, of little interest to the British, but the latter, Natal, occupied the coastal littoral east of the Drakensberg Mountains, another potentially strategic maritime location that the British could hardly allow to fall out of their control. In 1843, a naval expedition was sent to occupy Port Natal, the future Durban, and the territory was annexed and declared a British colony.

This, then, set the stage for the political evolution of the subcontinent of South Africa. The British acknowledged the existence of the Boer republics, and under certain conditions, the British even recognized their independence. Nonetheless, the British retained an unspoken option on both territories, should circumstances ever require it.

For the time being, however, the two republics had nothing much of strategic or economic interest to offer, so they were left to develop along their own preferred lines. The British, on the whole, were interested in the territory only from a naval/strategic perspective, and so long as the key ports lay in British hands, the interior could languish under Boer control indefinitely.

**A map of the British Cape Colony (blue), Transvaal (green), the Orange Free State (orange), and the Natal (red)**

It is interesting to note that as parties of Trekboere began crossing the Orange River and heading across the open plains of what would in future be the Orange Free State, they encountered a land almost empty of population. By then, the Mfecane had swept across the land, and where once the Basotho tribes had roamed the land, only a handful of starving fugitive groups survived. This, once again, lent the impression that the land was unoccupied, which was used to justify its takeover.

Between 1835 and 1837, six individual treks left the Eastern Cape, and by 1840, roughly 6,000 Boer, about a fifth of the rural population, had abandoned the Cape. Inevitably, the vanguard of the migration encountered the two great native societies of the day, the Zulu and the amaNdebele. Beating the Zulu in combat was one thing, but dealing with the British was an altogether different proposition. The British, alarmed at the possibility of losing the strategic port of Port Natal, annexed the territory in 1843 and declared it a British colony. The independence of Transvaal, however, was ratified in 1853 via the Treaty of Sand River with the British, upon the key provisos that the rights of British subjects would be respected and slavery would not be practiced. The Orange Free State, although initially anxious to remain under British administration as the Orange River Sovereignty, was handed over by the British in 1854 under similar terms.

This was the essential character of South Africa by the second half of the 19th century. The subcontinent south of the Limpopo River was locked in an unhappy marriage of two opposing territorial concepts. There were the two British colonies of the Cape and Natal, and the two independent Boer republics of Transvaal and the Orange Free State.

**Mineral Discoveries and the Countdown to War**

In the mid-19th century, the British were content to let the Boer have their republics. At that time, South Africa was a strategic portion of the British Empire solely in regard to naval and merchant shipping. The Cape was essential to British communications with India and Australia, and it could not be allowed to fall into unfriendly hands. Beyond that, however, South Africa appeared to have little to offer the British Empire in the way of economic interests, serving mostly as an agricultural waystation and a rather unimportant imperial backwater.

People located around the Cape continued to live under an extremely liberal constitution, and they had, under both Dutch and British administration, always been liberal. In 1872, the Cape Colony was granted responsible government, which meant in effect that the people enjoyed administrative and legislative independence under loose imperial control. This led to a revised constitution, under which the franchise was "color blind" insofar as it was open to every man over 21 regardless of race, color, or creed so long as he could meet certain educational and property qualifications. The participation of blacks in the electoral process was actively encouraged, and it is perhaps fair to say that the Cape offered, at that time, the most liberal and open political environment anywhere in the world.

Then, in 1866, a man named Erasmus Jacobs unearthed an interesting looking pebble on the banks of the Orange River. This proved to be a 22-carat diamond, and from that moment on, South Africa emerged as the principal theater of capital adventure and war across the entire scope of the British Empire. The diamond pipeline that would soon form the mining settlement of Kimberley was located in an undefined area on the borders of the Northern Cape and the Orange Free State that was more Orange Free State than Cape. However, thanks to the highly questionable decision made by a British commission of inquiry, it was declared to be part of the Cape and thus British. In short order, the subsequent bonanza attracted English-speaking immigrants and British capital from across the imperial spectrum.

One of those joining the diamond rush was an 18-year-old youth by the name of Cecil John Rhodes. Rhodes came the diamond fields in 1871, a tubercular and asthmatic youth sent out to the colonies in the hopes of avoiding an early death. In South Africa, the weakling certainly became a man, and in Kimberley, that man became a titan. Rhodes was a passionate imperialist who believed with utter conviction in the God-given right of the English-speaking races to rule. While this might sit uncomfortably in the milieu of modern thinking, at the time it was based on a profound sense of British manifest destiny. As Rhodes put it, "I contend that we are the first race in the world and that the more of the world we inhabit the better it is for the human race."

**Rhodes**

While this was certainly hubris, it was also based on the fundamental "civilizing" mission of the British Empire, a concept widely subscribed to and supported as a British duty, referred to in other quarters as the "White Man's Burden." The idea of the White Man's Burden emerged as a philanthropic mood began to define (and justify) the British sense of imperial mission. In the aftermath of the slave trade, large areas of Africa lay in ruins, and it became a popular British idea that the role of the empire, at least in part, was to repair this state of affairs. Rhodes tended to define it as "philanthropy plus five per cent," which was certainly the ideal.

The essence of Rhodes' vision was to unite all the territories of Africa under the Union Jack. By then, that view was made complex if not impossible by the French, Belgians, and Germans, who had for their parts seized control of much of west and central Africa. Rhodes modfieid his dream down to establishing a rail and telegraph link from British South Africa to British North Africa, or his famous Cape to Cairo concept.

As a part of the same general idea, Rhodes also pictured the unification of South Africa under the Union Jack, which to his mind, and to most right-thinking imperial strategists, would be the only practical way to realize the full economic potential of the region. No matter how logical it was or not, an idea like that would likely attract the utter scorn of the Boer, and to achieve it, if it was possible to achieve at all, would require a great deal of skill, considerable diplomatic maneuver, and no small amount of money. To start the process, Rhodes entered politics, taking his seat in the Cape parliament as a junior backbencher in 1881. He was just 28, but he was already extremely wealthy, and his objective was simply to win the trust of the Cape Dutch community, those Dutch-speaking citizens of the Cape who had not fled British rule. Rhodes sensed that if he could convince them, they would ease the anxieties of the Boer and persuade them of the obvious advantages of British rule.

The next major South African milestone was the discovery of gold. In 1886, in the Witwatersrand region of the Transvaal, the world's richest deposits of gold were unearthed, triggering a gold rush that would transform the demographic character of the Transvaal and the economic complexion of South Africa entirely. Unlike the diamond discovery, however, South African gold lay indisputably in the Boer republic, and no amount of creative map drawing could change that. Still, British capital flooded into the Transvaal alongside waves of English-speaking fortune seekers originating from as far afield as Australia and the United States, not to mention Britain itself.

The Boer themselves did not directly engage in mining, but they heavily taxed British mining activities and held monopolies on such vital commodities as dynamite. The Boer had something of a love-hate relationship with gold, which brought in a phenomenal amount of money but also introduced a great many English-speaking immigrants whose capital influence and numbers had the potential to overwhelm the Boer population. While it remained a cherished ideal to exist beyond the reach of British interference, gold brought the British into the Transvaal and gave them a reason to intrigue for political rights and representation. This presented a major conundrum for the Transvaal leadership, for if they were to grant the foreigners access to the local franchise, any hope of perpetual Boer sovereignty would be obliterated overnight.

This, then, was the Boer's dilemma. The *Uitlanders*, as the foreigners were known, agitated for relief from taxation and access to the franchise, which the Boer, for obvious reasons, simply would not grant. As a result, war, which up to this point had been a possibility, now became an inevitability. From the point of view of the British, it became simply a matter of contriving a viable reason to fight.

As the British and Boer moved toward war, the British found themselves fighting the Zulu. In 1873, King Mpande kaSenzangakhona, king of the Zulu Nation since 1840, died and left his son Cetshwayo to assume the throne. Mpande was a half-brother of Shaka and Dingane, both of whom preceded him as kings of the Zulu Nation, thus making Cetshwayo related to Shaka by blood. Per custom, Cetshwayo erected a new capital (Ulundi, which still stands today in KwaZulu-Natal Province), expanded his army (readopting many of Shaka's methods abandoned by his father), and equipped his *impi* with European muskets, something previous kings had frowned upon in order to maintain Shaka's reforms. Cetshwayo then banished European missionaries from Zululand and was also rumored to have incited other native African groups to rebel against the Boers in Transvaal.

**A photograph of Cetshwayo taken in London in 1884**

**Cetshwayo in 1875**

   In December 1878, representatives of the British government, who may have been acting largely without authority, delivered an ultimatum to 11 Zulu chiefs under Cetshwayo telling him to disband his armies and accept British authority. This had followed three dispatches on October 17, November 21, and December 18 from Sir Michael Hicks Beach (who replaced Carnarvon as Secretary of State for the Colonies in November), stating in no uncertain terms that war with the Zulu was to be avoided and a British invasion of Zululand was prohibited. Beach had written, "The fact is that matters in Eastern Europe and India...wore so serious an aspect that we cannot have a Zulu war in addition to other greater and too possible troubles."[5]  Since the ultimatum was tantamount to relinquishing his throne and abandoning his people, Cetshwayo refused to obey and ordered his troops to prepare to defend their country "only if attacked" and not to carry the

---

[5]   Colenso, Frances E. *History of the Zulu War and Its Origin*. Page 258.

war beyond Zululand. He even directed his soldiers to avoid killing any invaders other than British soldiers.

On January 11, 1879, a British force of 5,000 soldiers under Lieutenant General Frederick Augustus Thesiger, 2nd Baron Chelmsford, invaded Zululand, reportedly without authorization from the British Government. Chelmsford had already underestimated the Zulu before fighting them, writing back in July 1878, "If I am called upon to conduct operations against them, I shall strive to be in a position to show them how hopelessly inferior they are to us in fighting power, altho' numerically stronger."

**Chelmsford**

However, even before his men fought the Zulu, Chelmsford found out how difficult it was just to travel around the region. It took him more than a week to move his army a dozen miles, and on the night of January 20 he made camp on a hill called Isandlwana. On the morning of January 22, he sent a majority of his forces south to find the main Zulu force, but he had not properly reconnoitered the ground and had no idea that 20,000 Zulu warriors were actually to the north. About 1,700 British soldiers were surprised that morning by the Zulu warriors, who wrecked the British center, annihilated its camp, and inflicted about 1,300 casualties on them. One British officer described the scene, "In a few seconds we distinctly saw the guns fired again, one after the other, sharp. This was done several times - a pause, and then a flash – flash! The sun was shining on the camp at the time, and then the camp looked dark, just as if a shadow was passing over it. The guns did not fire after that, and in a few minutes all the tents had disappeared." A Zulu warrior described the same dark phenomenon; it turned out there was a solar eclipse occurring at the climax of the battle.

**An illustration of the Battle of Isandlwana in the Illustrated London News and The Graphic**

The British public was outraged at the idea that the finest soldiers in the world could be beat by Africans wielding spears, but Chelmsford had a powerful patron: Queen Victoria herself. Chelmsford found other scapegoats, and he also pointed to the action at Rorke's Drift the same day as the decisive defeat, in which only about 150 British soldiers had resisted an overwhelming number of Zulu warriors for hours. Chelmsford was recalled to London several months later, and Queen Victoria recorded what he told her in an audience that September: "Ld. Chelmsford said no doubt poor Col. Durnford had disobeyed orders, in leaving the camp as he did... Ld. Chelmsford knew nothing, Col. Durnford never having sent any message to say he was in danger... This much is clear to me: viz. that it was not his fault, but that of others, that this surprise at Sandlwana took place... I told Ld. Chelmsford he had been blamed by many, and even by the Government, for commencing the war without sufficient cause. He replied that he believed it to have been quite inevitable; that if we had not made war when we did, we should have been attacked and possibly overpowered."

Chelmsford had lied outright to the queen, but at that point it didn't much matter anymore. The British managed to gain the upper hand through strategic movements, including outflanking the Zulu, who were not accustomed to such military maneuvers. On July 4, 1879 at the Battle of Ulundi, 16,000 British and 7,000 native allies under Chelmsford proved insurmountable. Though

Cetshwayo attempted to negotiate a peace treaty prior to this battle, Chelmsford was not open to negotiations; Cetshwayo's capital city of Ulundi was captured and partially torched.

**Charles Edwin Fripp's painting of the Battle of Isandlwana**

After the Battle of Ulundi, the Zulu Army dispersed, and most of the leading chiefs tendered their submission to the British. Cetshwayo became a fugitive, but on August 28, 1879, he was finally captured and exiled, first to Cape Town and then to London. He would not return until 1883, but when he did return, he merely assumed a role that was little more than figurehead. Ironically, it was Chelmsford who was rewarded most as a result of the war, thanks to the queen, who made him a full general and bestowing other honors on him, including making him Lieutenant of the Tower of London.

Once Cetshwayo was captured, the British divided the Zulu Empire into 13 "kinglets." By 1882, however, differences between two Zulu factions – one supporting Cetshwayo and the other supporting rival chief UZibhebhu - erupted into a blood-feud civil war. Attempting to restore order over these tribal wars, which were coming dangerously close to white settlements, in 1883 the British reinstated Cetshwayo as king of Zululand, but that only exacerbated matters. With the aid of Boer mercenaries, Chief UZibhebhu initiated an uprising in protest of Cetshwayo's reinstatement and attacked Cetshwayo's new *kraal* in Ulundion on July 22, 1883. Wounded during the attack, Cetshwayo managed to escape to Nkandla in the KwaZulu-Natal forest. After pleas from Resident Commissioner Sir Melmoth Osborne, Cetshwayo moved to the European settlement of Eshowe, the oldest European settlement in Zululand, where he died a few months later on February 8, 1884 at the age of 57 (or 60 by some accounts). He left his 15 year old son

Dinuzulu to assume the throne, and Zulu infighting would continue for years, until Zululand was fully absorbed into the British colony of Natal, subsequently ceasing to exist.

Secretary Carnarvon had hoped to achieve a confederation by diplomatic means, but it ultimately took the British until 1877 to annex the disintegrating Transvaal, and war was required to subdue the Xhosa (1877-1878), the Pedi (1877-1879), the Zulu (1879), and the Sotho (1880). Most significantly, the results of these military actions was the breaking of the economic and political backs of the two most powerful southern Africa states, the Pedi and Zulu Empires. The Pedi lost their cattle and land, while the Zulu were dispersed into 13 separate and competing units.

**The Boer War**

Prior to the discovery of gold in the Transvaal, the republic was impoverished, and as a consequence, vulnerable to British expansionist policies. On April 12, 1877, two years before the Anglo-Zulu War, the British had actually annexed the Transvaal in a bloodless and peaceful operation led by none other than Theophilus Shepstone. From there, it was widely assumed by the British that they could bring about the submission of the Orange Free State.

As it turned out, the generally peaceful reception of British rule in the Transvaal was dangerously deceptive. A majority of the Boer remained deeply inimical to the British and any presumption of the absorption of the Transvaal into the British Empire. Popular resistance simmered for the next few years, until, on December 20, 1880, a brief war broke out. Known as the First Anglo-Boer War, it caught the British by surprise, and in the course of a few weeks, sovereignty of the Transvaal went back to the Boer.

The matter was temporarily shelved as the frenzy of the gold rush washed over the Transvaal, and its economy was radically transformed. The Transvaal was now no longer impoverished but awash with gold revenue, and it was arming itself. Nonetheless, the question of British sovereignty over all of South Africa continued to preoccupy the metropolitan political establishment, and thanks to the sudden and meteoric wealth of the region, that preoccupation steadily grew.

A large part of British anxiety over the continued independence of the Transvaal lay in the sudden proximity of the Germans. In 1885, the German Empire annexed the territory of Damaraland, which would eventually become the German colony of South West Africa and later become Namibia. By then, the leaders of the various nations believed that the different countries' global expansion would heighten tensions among the Europeans and bring about a global war. To deal with that eventuality, the security of British strategic interests in southern Africa was vital, and the weak link in that regard was the Boer.

The British and everyone else understood that the Boer's hatred would possibly lead them to ally with Britain's enemies. There was also something of a natural ideological alliance between the Boer and the Germans, so there was every reason to suppose that a political and security alliance would soon follow. It is questionable how much better an alliance with Germany would be to an alliance with Britain, but that certainly appeared to be the direction that things were going, and if that happened, it would certainly position the Germans to take over the entirety of South Africa and its goldfields, diamond fields, and strategic ports. This was something the British could obviously not tolerate, and if the Boer could not be induced to peacefully accept British sovereignty, they would have to do so under force of arms.

It was not only British capitalists and industrialists who financed the Transvaal mining industry, but largely British-affiliated workers who ran the mines and attended to the innumerable peripheral and support industries associated with the mines. Most of this took place in the thriving and chaotic mining city of Johannesburg, and in due course, Johannesburg became an English speaking region. For its part, the central government of the Transvaal, located in the capital city of Pretoria, levied heavy taxes against the mining industry and ran several lucrative and questionable monopolies over such vital commodities as explosives.

All of this was extremely lucrative, but at the same time, the Transvaal Boer, led by an aging patriarch named President Paul Kruger, resolutely resisted calls by various expatriate lobbies (the Boer referred to the non-Boer émigré community as Uitlanders, or Foreigners) to provide limits on taxation, and representation commensurate with that taxation. The Uitlander population, by the latter half of the 19th century, had grown in numbers and capital influence to such a degree that a free grant of voting rights would have meant, in practical terms, an Uitlander government in the Transvaal. Gone in an instant would be the cherished Boer ideal of independence, sovereignty, and freedom from British domination. Kruger could simply not countenance this.

**Kruger**

By now, Rhodes occupied the office of Prime Minister of the Cape Colony, and with vast wealth at his disposal, he was in a position of enormous local power. Sometime during 1895, he formed a covert alliance with the Conservative British Colonial Secretary, Joseph Chamberlain, who happened to share his vision for a united South Africa, albeit for different reasons. Rhodes was a capitalist and a visionary, and there was always a strong strain of ideology that ran through his thinking. Chamberlain, on the other hand, was a political strategist, and he was concerned with the proximity of the Germans, the potential of a German/Boer alliance, and the likely implications this had on Britain's strategic position in Africa. Chamberlain also worried about a wider European war being inevitable.

**Chamberlain**

   While carefully camouflaging his involvement, Chamberlain tacitly supported the development of a plot in South Africa, devised by Rhodes and supported by Rhodes' local network. In essence, the plot involved leveraging Uitlander discontent in the Transvaal to create a coup d'état. Rhodes would provide the arms and the money, and he would orchestrate the start of the coup. That trigger would take the form of a mounted force of some 600 men, drawn from the colonial militia of his territory of Rhodesia. At a predetermined time, the Uitlanders in Johannesburg would rise in rebellion, and the armed force, led by a man named Leander Starr Jameson, would ride into the city, take control of the gold mines, and then engineer the collapse of the Transvaal government.

**Jameson**

As it turned out, Rhodes made one major miscalculation, and it was simply that wealthy men are seldom predisposed to revolution. A great deal of hue and cry was generated, and a rather amateurish organization of the plot ensured that the Boers were well-informed of every detail, so that when the raid was launched on New Year's Eve of 1896, the Uitlanders manifestly declined to place themselves in harm's way and the raiders were met by a fully armed Boer reception party.

As Julius Caesar once remarked, if one must break the law, then do so to seize power, but in all other cases, obey it. Rhodes failed to seize power, so he simply broke the law. Chamberlain, the complicit British Colonial Secretary naturally distanced himself from the planning and denied all knowledge, leaving Rhodes to bear the consequences alone. The raiders were extradited to Britain to face trial, while Rhodes was eventually removed from all of his major business interests and forced to resign as Prime Minister of the Cape Colony. He never achieved the same level of power and influence again.

**An 1896 depiction of the arrest of Jameson**

Although it was an abject failure, the Jameson Raid set in motion a chain of events that would lead to war. The Uitlander crisis continued to ferment, and the British authorities in South Africa, supported by Whitehall, initiated negotiations with the government of the Transvaal over the question of Uitlander rights and liberties in the republic. These negotiations were somewhat disingenuous since the British were looking to instigate some sort of conflict, and in due course, as he was backed into a corner, President Kruger issued an ultimatum for the removal of British troops from the borders of the republic. The British press bellowed with derisive mirth at the audacity of it, as did the Victorian public, and the ultimatum was ignored.

Thus, on October 11, 1899, war was declared.

On the eve of the war, the British armed presence in South Africa was extremely limited. The Boer, on the other hand, had been covertly arming and organizing for some time. As a result, by the time the war started, it was estimated by British intelligence that some 32,000 fighting men were on call in the Transvaal alone. These were supported by a modern and well equipped artillery division, the Staats Artillerie, an extremely functional police force, the Zuid-Afrikaansche Republiek Politie (ZARP), and a widespread and effective intelligence network. As Chamberlain had suspected, the Germans were sympathetic to the Boer, and almost all of the Boer war materiel and equipment were sourced from Germany. This cooperation fell short of a formal alliance, but Boer fighters were nonetheless armed with the latest Mauser Model 93/95 rifles, and plenty of Boer artillery had been manufactured by the Germans.

The Boer military structure was based on a commando system that had evolved as a civil defense in response to generations of frontier and border wars with black South African tribes. A permanent official within the community, known as a Veldkornet, dealt with what formal organization there was, and he both commanded and summoned the commandos when they were needed. Boer commandos, therefore, comprised an informal mounted infantry, usually highly mobile, and they embraced community-based units that consisted of all able-bodied men, urban and rural, within any given area. These men were expected to serve at a moment's notice if the call came.

The weakness in this arrangement was command. As with all informal militias, volunteers could be led but never driven. Command was based not on a rigid hierarchy, as was the case with the British Army, but by the consent of the majority, so tactics and strategy were agreed to by consensus, which inevitably resulted in a weak and variable chain of command.

At the outbreak of war, command of Boer forces resided in the hands of a 68 year old patriarch by the name of Piet Joubert, whose military experience was informal and whose command style was cautious. His combat history had been mainly during the "Kaffir Wars," the wars of pacification fought against native tribes. There certainly were younger men within the command structure, and many with more progressive ideas, but it was the elders who tended to hold sway within the military council. Consequently, the immediate strategy that evolved was cautious and conservative.

**Joubert**

Cautious ideology or not, the military situation at the onset very much favored the Boer. The British could rely on just a small garrison of a few thousand imperial troops and a collection of regionally organized colonial militias. The younger men within the Boer leadership, among them a brilliant young lawyer by the name of Jan Christiaan Smuts (then the Transvaal state attorney) and a charismatic farmer by the name of Louis Botha, both urged a rapid seizure of the key ports in order to prevent the landing of a British expeditionary force, which would inevitably occur at some point. This was undoubtedly a logical strategy, and had it been followed, it is possible that what many saw as an inevitable Boer defeat might have been avoided.

**Smuts**

**Smuts and Boer guerrillas in 1901**

**Botha**

At the same time, there were many within the higher echelons of Boer leadership, most notably Jan Smuts, who did not see much hope of an ultimate military victory for the Boer. The integration of the Boer republics into the British network of overseas territories was in some respects inevitable, and the overwhelming power of the British Empire somewhat precluded any hope of the British truly being defeated. What Smuts and others saw as more likely was a situation where war, in the Clausewitzian sense of the word, would be deployed as an instrument of politics. It was a question of under what terms and conditions the republics would submit to British superintendentship, and what could be decided by war.

Others, of course, did not see the situation in quite so nuanced a form. Anti-British sentiment was almost a religion in the republics, and among the mid-level command, ignorance of the outside world and a general lack of strategic understanding meant that many believed it was a simple question of victory or defeat.

From the beginning, the British moved wisely. The Jameson Raid had originated from the British protectorate of Bechuanaland, the modern day Botswana, and the British gambled that a build-up of forces in the same region would play on Boer paranoia, resulting in a deployment of forces away from the main strategic ports in the Cape and in Natal. The British strategy was to draw Boer forces into the north and northeast of the Transvaal, and from there the British would defend two key settlements, the diamond mining town of Kimberley and the railway depot of Mafeking. This would draw the Boer into pointless sieges that would divert and engage a disproportional amount of Boer manpower, and so long as the sieges were maintained, that manpower would be diverted away from more potentially productive targets.

When war broke out, this is precisely what happened, and the sieges of Kimberley and Mafeking began by mid-October. However, on October 12, a day after the declaration, 21,000 Boer horsemen also surged out of the Transvaal and the Orange Free State into Natal, where they laid siege to the British garrison town of Ladysmith, which most analysts agree was the signature Boer strategic blunder of the war. Without a doubt, had that force bypassed Ladysmith and thereby isolated the garrison by simply sealing road and rail access, it could have concentrated its main effort on the port town of Durban, Natal. That would have made British landings far more difficult. At the same time, had the temptation to lay siege to Mafeking and Kimberley been resisted, and the men and artillery so preoccupied been directed to Cape Town and Port Elizabeth, the Cape might also have been secured.

**A picture of Boer troops in a trench outside Mafeking**

The sieges of Kimberley and Mafeking were for the most part static, while Ladysmith, the more famous of the three, was much more dynamic.

The commander of British troops in South Africa was Sir Redvers Buller, a veteran of the subcontinent and many other African colonial conflicts. When the war started, Buller was dispatched from England, and he arrived in South Africa to assume his command at the end of October 1899. By then, a mixed force of some 15,000 British troops, the Natal Field Force, had been diverted to Natal from various locations and had landed under the command of Lieutenant General Sir George White. In the expectation of a Boer movement against the Natal ports, White had been advised not to deploy his troops too far inland, but upon taking command, he discovered that his immediate subordinate, General Sir Penn Symons, had already pushed advance units to two points in the Natal interior. The first of these was the garrison town of Ladysmith, located 60 miles inland of Durban, and the second was the coal mining town of Dundee, a further 25 miles northeast of Ladysmith.

**Buller and his wife**

**White**

Surrounded by hills, Dundee became the site of the first major action of the war.[6] The *Battle of Talana Hill* took place on October 20, 1899, as Boer forces occupied a prominent hill overlooking the town, and opened the action with a largely ineffectual artillery barrage aimed at the British camp. The character of the British response was direct, with a full frontal infantry advance covered by reasonably accurate artillery fire advancing directly against Boer positions. It was a punishing advance for the British, who paid dearly for their first victory, losing some 446 men in the action, including General Sir Penn Symons himself who received a fatal rifle shot in the stomach.

As advance British troops closed in on the summit of the hill, the Boer simply mounted their horses and galloped away, regrouping at a point called Elandslaagte. This cut off the British retreat to the main force in Ladysmith, which would prove to be the pattern in many of the preliminary battles that followed.

The opening stages of the war were conventional, insofar as the Boer moved in large formations, utilizing supply columns and artillery. Even still, they were significantly more mobile than the British. British columns were monolithic, and their tactical maneuvers were ponderous and predictable. In this regard, the Boers enjoyed an initial advantage.

Meanwhile, a second action was fought soon afterwards as the British attacked Boer positions at Elandslaagte to clear the lines. In what came to be known as the Battle of Elandslaagte, the

---

[6] The *Battle of Kraaipan* in the Northern Cape occurred a week earlier, which was a smaller action, and which preceded the Siege of Mafeking.

British, commanded by Major General John French, scattered the Boer. General White, assessing the situation from his command room in Ladysmith, was convinced that a much larger concentration of Boer was massing to hit the advanced column, so he ordered a rapid retreat. Given that the British won a tactical victory at Elandslaagte, this had about it the flavor of an overly hasty retreat, and it immediately squandered any advantage gained. As the column entered the precincts of Ladysmith a few days later, the Boer simply closed in behind them, and positioning their siege guns on the surrounding high ground, they began to lay down a carpet of fire.

General White, in a rather ill-conceived response, sent out a strong foot and mounted force under orders to take the Boer artillery positions, but the attack was almost immediately broken against the entrenched Boer forces and an enfilade of witheringly accurate Boer musketry. This became known as the Battle of Ladysmith, and it ushered in a period of disastrous British reverses that would mark the beginning of the British counter-offensive. The British seemed to consistently underestimate the mobile fighting capabilities and the superb marksmanship of individual Boer combatants, and in long-range engagements over open ground, the advantage almost always went the Boer's way.

**British soldiers at the Battle of Ladysmith**

At this point in the conflict, Boer morale and cohesion were very high. They were well-armed, capably led on a detachment level, and well-mounted. British troops, on the other hand, with a command element still somewhat reliant on the tactics of the last war, deployed set-piece advances over open ground, or in the face of entrenched positions that were easily targeted and cut up by a mobile and elusive enemy. The British were armed with a state-of-the-art rifle, the .303 Lee Metford, that was capable of a high degree of accuracy and a high rate of fire, but these advantages were not properly utilized. Perhaps the only real utilitarian advance that the British

Army had made since the last major war in South Africa, fought against the Zulu, was to abandon the ubiquitous redcoat, which would have been nothing less than a joy to Boer marksmen as the hapless British troopers marched in open formation across the battlefield. British troops now adopted khaki, which proved to be a far more practical uniform for the African veld, but their battlefield tactics were still slower to evolve.

It is also perhaps worth noting that the British Expeditionary Force that set sail soon afterwards, and which would eventually number upwards of 240,000 men, included numerous colonial militias and detachments from Canada, New Zealand and Australia. They joined numerous local rough-rider style commandoes, and they introduced to the tactical rulebook of the British Army an entirely new concept of warfare. As the Boer fought an increasingly mobile campaign, utilizing marksmanship and horsemanship in combination with local knowledge, these smaller imperial units responded in kind, developing many of the ground rules of future guerrilla warfare.

In the wake of the Battle of Ladysmith, the British attack column returned to Ladysmith having suffered 140 men killed, many more wounded, and some 1,000 captured. After that, the Siege of Ladysmith began.

By the time the siege closed in on Ladysmith, the sieges of Kimberley and Mafeking had been in effect for almost a month, and the stresses of siege life had already begun to tell in both places. Regular artillery bombardments and food shortages were the main problems, and as the sieges wore on, these stresses amplified. Eventually, however, siege life settled into a predictable routine on both sides, and permeable lines allowed for some back-and-forth movement of dispatches and personnel. The Siege of Mafeking, commanded by the legendary Colonel Robert Baden-Powell, was perhaps the most isolated of all, and conditions were the most spartan, but in all instances, a high degree of creativity came into play. There was plenty of daring in the periodic breaking of the sieges, and even some gentlemanly fair play in the celebration of events and holidays.

**Baden-Powell**

Trapped in Kimberley at the time of the siege was Cecil John Rhodes, whose mining interests were mainly in that city. Rhodes, in keeping with his nature, frequently attempted to usurp the authority of the military commander, Lieutenant Colonel Robert Kekewich, who periodically threatened Rhodes with arrest over his constant meddling. Kimberley was a large mining settlement, so numerous industrial workshops were available to improvise weapons and protections, including an armored train. On the whole, the residents of Kimberley survived the experience without too great a hardship.

**Kekewich**

Ladysmith, however, was where the attention of the British Empire was mostly focused. Commanding the Boer forces was the young and charismatic field commander Louis Botha. The world would hear a great deal of Louis Botha in future years, and eventually he would emerge as the first Prime Minister of the Transvaal, and then of the Union of South Africa. He would ultimately become one of the most widely respected imperial statesmen of the 20th century. For the time being, however, he was just 37 years old, but a dynamic and gifted tactical commander.

Botha had already proved himself in the field, but the real test would come when he faced the imperious and overconfident General Buller. Buller had by then landed in Cape Town, and he was busy organizing his expeditionary force, which included an army corps of three divisions. His original intention had been to march directly northwards from Cape Town to Pretoria, taking the Orange Free State Capital of Bloemfontein en route, but the sieges complicated this, so he was forced upon arrival to modify his plan. One division was therefore sent north under the command of Lieutenant General Lord Paul Methuen to relieve the garrisons at Kimberley and Mafeking, another smaller force was sent to contain any possible uprising of Boer in the Cape, and he personally led the largest detachment by sea to Port Natal, from where he would push overland towards Ladysmith.

This monumental deployment began what has since come to be known in British military lore as Black Week. The large, heavily supported British columns immediately began to run afoul of mobile Boer commandos, and from December 10-15, the British suffered several shocking defeats.

The first of these was the Battle of Stormberg, fought on December 10, where 135 British troops were killed and 600 were captured. Next came the Battle of Magersfontein on December 11, in which 14,000 British troops advanced on Kimberley and were thrown back at the cost of 120 killed and 690 wounded. The efforts to relieve Kimberley and Mafeking were failing miserably.

The lowest point of Black Week came on December 15, 1899, when Buller, leading a column of 21,000 men, came up against a smaller force of 8,000 Transvaal Boer commanded by General Botha. Buller landed in Durban on December 6, and with surprising efficiency, was very quickly on the move. News reached him en route of the defeats at Stormberg and Magersfontein, which simply added to his impatience to deal promptly with Ladysmith in order that he could turn his attention to the wider theatre. A major obstacle to be negotiated, however, was the Tugela River, flowing off the eastern slopes of the Drakensberg and entering the Indian Ocean some 70 miles north of Durban. This barred his way, and under any circumstances, it was a formidable obstacle and a superb defensive barrier for the Boer. Buller made a direct approach on the river in the direction of the small town of Colenso, located 20 miles or so south of Ladysmith. The landscape was open, with areas of high ground scattered here and there upon which Boer reconnaissance groups carefully plotted his advance. On the opposing bank, the Boers were dug in, ready to contest the crossing.

The Battle of Colenso was not only a confused and bloody action, replete with the desperate heroism so typical of British military lore – four Victoria Crosses were awarded – but it also demonstrated the same stultifying lack of tactical creativity that was a trademark feature of Victorian warfare. Ultimately, Buller's division was thwarted in its effort to cross, and it was driven back with heavy casualties. British losses ran to 143 killed, 756 wounded, and 220 captured. The battlefield consisted largely of open ground, which gave the Boer a virtually unrestricted field of fire, and notwithstanding punishing artillery duels back and forth across the river, efforts to move infantry across the river simply proved too costly. A portion of the high ground – a hill known as Hlangwane – was occupied by the Boer, and it commanded the battlefield. So long as this was held, the Boer held the advantage.

**A picture of part of the battleground**

The British weren't the only ones making mistakes. The Boer did not follow-up these impressive tactical victories, allowing the British to withdraw, regroup and reorganize. Over the next few weeks, Buller received steady reinforcements, and as he waited, he modified his plan. He would now move 30 miles upstream and cross the river at two points. Once he established a bridgehead, he would move his force across in order to complete the 20 miles to Ladysmith. Crucially, he intended to attack and neutralize a heavily defended Boer position on a hill known as Spion Kop, guarding the left flank of his advance. Spion Kop, at 1,410 feet, was the commanding feature of the local landscape, and with an artillery battery positioned on top, the British would effectively command the approaches to Ladysmith.

The crossing was achieved without particular difficulty, but it was during the assault on Spion Kop that things once again began to unravel. This was perhaps the most iconic battle of Buller's advance, the Battle of Spion Kop, which has been made even more famous by the fact that the Indian barrister Mohandas K. Gandhi served on the battlefield as a stretcher bearer, as a member of the Natal Indian Ambulance Corps.

**Boer forces at Spion Kop**

The topography of Spion Kop resembles an extended "L," with the tail facing north and the highest point at the apex. Five distinct peaks or promontories mark the summit, and the Boer held the highest. On the evening of January 23, 1900, under cover of darkness and obscured by mist, the British climbed the hill and expelled a small Boer detachment from what they assumed was the summit. However, the daylight revealed that they had only occupied the lowest of the five summits, an acre-sized plateau exposed on three sides to Boer positions on higher ground. Entrenchment was difficult because of the hard ground, and 1,000 or more British troops thus found themselves exposed on three sides to enemy fire.

**A map of the 5 peaks**

Botha ordered his men to take the position before the British could move up their heavy guns. Heavy salvos of fire poured into the shallow British trenches, and casualties quickly began to mount. The Boer directed their artillery from adjacent positions, and accurate shelling added to the misery of the beleaguered British troops. Boer reinforcements then moved up and began hitting the British from the right flank. The commanding officer, Major General Edward Woodgate, was felled by a shard of shrapnel above his right eye, and his replacement, Colonel Malby Crofton, signaled the column commander, General Sir Charles Warren, by heliograph that without immediate reinforcements, all was lost. General Warren replied with the typical valor of a rear commander that the position must be held to the last. No surrender must be contemplated.

That night, the defenders held their position, absorbing dreadful casualties while tactical command gradually collapsed in the mounting chaos. Hours later, dawn rose on a scene of abject slaughter. Tormented by heat and thirst, low on ammunition, and still under withering fire, the surviving commander, Lieutenant Colonel Alexander Thorneycroft, continued to plead for permission to withdraw. In the end, in consultation with his fellow officers, Thorneycroft ordered a complete withdrawal on his own authority. "Better six good battalions safely down the hill than a bloody mop-up in the morning." He is reported to have later remarked. "I've done all I can, and I'm not going back."

**A picture of dead British soldiers on the battlefield**

Ironically, the Boer forces had also largely abandoned their positions, having reached their own conclusion that further defense was pointless. The fact that British defenses had also been abandoned was only accidentally discovered by two Boer Scouts, who probed the hilltop in the early afternoon and found British trenches manned only by the dead. The Boer quickly returned and hailed their victory. The British suffered 243 fatalities during the battle, most of which were buried in the trenches where they fell. Approximately 1,250 British were either wounded or captured. The Boer, on the other hand, lost just 68 men dead and 267 wounded.

Despite the setback, the sheer weight of British numbers prevailed, and Buller was able to throw a pontoon bridge across the Tugela. After that, a mass of British infantry bore down on Ladysmith, taking the last defended points of high ground along the way. The Siege of Ladysmith was lifted on February 27, 1900, having lasted for 118 days. Withstanding the siege and lifting it cost some 7,000 British casualties.

**John Henry Frederick Bacon's painting depicting the lifting of the siege at Ladysmith**

In time, the weight of British numbers prevailed over the sieges of Kimberley and Mafeking as well. The relief of Kimberley was achieved on February 15, 1900, and Mafeking was relieved on May 18.

Ironically, Buller would not be the commander who relieved Ladysmith, because his handling of the campaign came under considerable criticism, and he was relieved of overall command on December 23, 1899. He was replaced by General Sir Frederick Roberts, who arrived in Cape Town on January 10, 1900 with his second-in-command, General Lord Kitchener. They led an expeditionary force of some 50,000 men, supported by over 100 pieces of artillery.

The lifting of the sieges was a major psychological blow to the Boer, but perhaps even more so was an action that took place from February 18-27, known as the Battle of Paardeberg. The battle was fought along the banks of the Modder River about 20 miles east of Kimberley. At that battle, an army of 4,000 Boer, under the command of General Piet Cronjé, surrendered to the British, taking out of action 7% of the Boer forces.

Cronjé

**Roberts**

The series of Boer defeats that had led to the lifting of the three sieges, in conjunction with the debacle at Paardeberg, served to convince many that it would now be impossible to reasonably oppose an overwhelming British force consolidating to capture and occupy the republics. Inevitably, a defeatist mood began to creep into the ranks of the Boer commandos. These prognostications tended to be confirmed as Roberts began to rapidly advance north from the Cape to the Orange Free State, scattering Boer resistance ahead of an unopposed occupation of Bloemfontein on March 13, 1900. The tide certainly seemed to have turned. The Orange Free State was formally annexed to Britain on May 28 and renamed the Orange River Colony, after which it came under British military administration There seemed little now to hold back a lightning British advance on Pretoria.

On March 17, four days after the occupation of Bloemfontein, a meeting of the two state presidents and all of the senior commanders was held in the temporary capital of the Orange Free State, Kroonstad, located 60 miles north of Bloemfontein in the direction of Pretoria. Here it was acknowledged that attempting to counter Roberts' steamroller tactics by conventional methods was hopeless. The struggle to retain republican independence would continue, but the strategy and tactics used to achieve this would have to change. Instead of adopting a conventional defensive position to meet the British advance across a broad front, Boer forces would now be organized into smaller units, operating in a mobile configuration and no longer dependent on conspicuous supply columns. The objective would henceforth be to interdict British lines of communication, attack from the rear, and harass the British columns at every opportunity. The broad objective was simply to extend British forces, drain British resources, and eventually provoke a backlash in Britain that would lead to favorable conditions for peace.

It was agreed, therefore, that the republican forces would split up into four main commando groups. Upon the death of Joubert in March 1900, Botha had been appointed Commandant-General of Boer forces, and he would take as his sector the Eastern Transvaal, the modern day Mpumalanga Province of South Africa. Generals Christian de Wet and James Hertzog, both Free State men, would command that sector. General Christiaan Beyers would command the territories north of Pretoria, while the ageing but highly respected General Jacobus "Koos" de la Rey would take command of the western Transvaal. Second-in-command to Koos de la Rey was the 30 year old Smuts, who had until the abandonment of Pretoria served as State Attorney and was a rising star in the Boer leadership. He was a rare creature insofar as he had been born in the Cape, making him a British subject. Indeed, he had studied law at Christ's College, Cambridge, was a member of a British Bar Association, and was fully aware of British cultural and academic tradition. He was nonetheless committed to the preservation of the republics and had been a key aid to President Kruger during the tense negotiations with the British prior to the ultimatum. At the outbreak of war, he had remained in his cabinet position, but with the collapse of the government, he was naturally absorbed into the commandos at a senior rank, even though he had no prior military experience at all.

It is also important to note that the switching of tactics from conventional defensive stances to mobile offensive operations was only really possible once the older and more conservative Boer commanders had ceded authority for one reason or another to younger, more innovative men. General Christian de Wet would emerge as probably the most celebrated Boer guerrilla leader, but Botha, de la Rey, and Smuts would also go on to forge reputations as daring and innovative commanders during this period.

**De Wet**

**Hertzog**

In Pretoria, preparations began to be made to evacuate the government and prepare for an abandonment of the capital. President Kruger, 75 years old and in poor health, was put aboard a train, along with key members of his cabinet, and sent east towards Lourenço Marques, the main Portuguese East African port. Waiting for him there was the Dutch ship *Gelderland*, sent by Wilhelmina of the Netherlands to carry the Transvaal president away to safety. He would never return from his exile.

As Kruger's train steamed eastward, an enormous British expeditionary force advanced steadily on Pretoria in three parts, with two bearing up from the south commanded by General Lord Roberts himself and a third approaching from Natal under the command of Buller. By June 4, Lord Roberts had advanced to within just a few miles of the city. Johannesburg had been taken relatively easy on May 31, 1900, since it was already largely a British settled city, and after that Roberts set his sights on Pretoria. General John French, commanding the 1st Cavalry Brigade, was detached from the main force and sent west, via the small town of Krugersdorp, to circle around Pretoria and position himself to the north behind enemy lines.

This was an odd move under the circumstances. Had Roberts deployed French and his mobile force east of Pretoria instead of west, he would have been able to capture the vital Delagoa Bay railway line, upon which Kruger had recently slipped away, cutting off any further Boer retreat and blocking the obvious route of escape that the Boer defenders and leadership would take. In all likelihood, however, Roberts probably gave no consideration to the possibility that the Boer civil and military leadership would do anything other than surrender upon the occupation of Pretoria. In the British rulebook of warfare, the capture of the enemy's capital marked the end of the war, and the idea that the Boer would fall back on their time-honored principle of mobile warfare by abandoning their cities and taking to the countryside likely never occurred to him.

Behind the lines, however, de Wet had already begun mounting hit-and-run attacks against British positions, attacking from the rear, scoring several victories in quick succession, capturing quantities of arms and supplies, and inflicting significant casualties. Kitchener was promptly deployed south by Roberts to deal with this unexpected turn of events, but de Wet remained elusive. On the evening of June 12-13, Kitchener's guard unit was hit in a surprise raid, forcing Kitchener himself to flee the scene in his pajamas and take refuge in a nearby Yeomanry camp.

Kitchener of Khartoum. —Black and White

**Kitchener**

As this was going on, Roberts formally annexed the Transvaal on September 1, 1900, and satisfied that the war was effectively over, he handed over command of what he believed would be no more than extensive mopping up to his second-in-command, Lord Kitchener. He returned to England in late November to take up his new role as commander-in-chief of the British Army.

Unbeknownst to British leaders, the annexation of the two republics was premature. The British controlled the administrative centers, but the Boer held sway in the countryside. Roberts was still on the high seas heading back to England when the guerrilla war in South Africa escalated dramatically. On December 13, 1900, a Boer force commanded by de la Rey, Smuts, and Beyers surprised a British force at Nooitgedacht, west of Pretoria, and overran their camp. British losses were 109 killed, 186 wounded, and at least 368 taken prisoner, while the Boers lost only 32 killed and 46 wounded. This would form the pattern for the next few months.

In mid-December, Hertzog crossed the Orange River and entered the Cape Colony with a large force, intending to take the fight directly to the British in hopes of provoking a large-scale Boer rebellion in the Cape. In fact, the Cape Dutch had not and would not actively enter the war in big numbers. Some did on an individual basis, maybe 5,000 in total, but Hertzog's invasion did at least relieve the pressure elsewhere. Guerrilla activities elsewhere continued, with the western Transvaal, under de la Rey and Smuts, becoming arguably the most active region.

While they ramped up the guerrilla tactics, the Boer launched a parallel diplomatic offensive. The British, never popular in Europe, attempted to portray the ongoing action as the mopping up of limited resistance, while the Boer sought to counter this by assuring the international community, including the Americans, that they were still very much engaged in the struggle. Boer officials were sent to various European capitals and the United States in an effort to secure arbitration and support for a continuation of the struggle. However, while there was a great deal of expressed sympathy for the Boer's position, very little support or practical aid came about as a result of these efforts.

Perhaps one of the most noteworthy actions of the guerrilla phase of the war was General Smuts' invasion of the Cape Colony, which began early in September 1901 and followed up on Hertzog's unspectacular effort. This was undertaken for the same basic reason, but it proved much more successful, cementing Smuts' reputation as a gifted military commander and setting him on the path to attain one of the highest military offices in the British Empire.

Although the greater strategic objective of this ambitious raid was never achieved – the Cape Dutch still stayed out of the war – the episode was a remarkable tactical success insofar as some 350 mounted men successfully remained at large in the colony until the war was eventually concluded with a treaty. Although hounded relentlessly by British and loyal columns, it succeeded in remaining operational, raising its force to an eventual 4,000, and at times getting within 150 miles of Cape Town itself.

It soon became clear to Kitchener that he had been left with a job far greater than simply mopping up. A relatively small, mobile Boer force now had the British running around in circles across the vast spaces of South Africa, with no apparent intention of surrendering. What Kitchener was essentially confronting was the same kind of battle conditions that future counterinsurgency strategists would deal with in later African wars: an asymmetric military equation whereby the enemy enjoyed intimacy with the landscape and the broad sympathy of the non-combatant population. The campaign was now as much against the Boer as the almost limitless expanses of the South African Veld. The time-honored use of mass maneuver was irrelevant, and an entirely new strategy was required.

The first consideration was Boer support and supply. Now largely estranged from formal weapons procurement, the commandos were increasingly dependent on captured weapons and supplies. For this, Kitchener introduced severe penalties, including summary execution for any Boer combatants captured wearing British Army uniforms or using British equipment and weapons. That proved to have a minor impact; since they came from a largely agrarian population, almost every Boer fighter in the field was connected to a farm or rural homestead.

Since the Boer commandos were typically deployed on or near their home districts, a movement to and from the home front and the front-line was ongoing. Kitchener, therefore, conceived very quickly the advantage of cutting off this avenue of support. In fact, Roberts had previously ordered the destruction of rebel Boer farms in the Cape quite early on during his inland advance, but this was largely punitive rather than preventative, and also perhaps for the purpose of looting livestock. He regarded such targets as legitimate since Boer farms supplied the commandos with food, fodder for their horses, information with regard to British troop movements, and medical care to the wounded. Thanks to this, Kitchener was offered a precedent for a much wider implementation of the program, which is precisely what he did.

The British scorched earth policy went into effect piecemeal, but it quickly gathered intensity, and ultimately some 30,000 Boer farms and homesteads were burned or torched, with the additional destruction of associated black homesteads. This resulted in the devastation of over 100,000 homes. Alongside this, 40 towns and villages of various sizes were razed to the ground. As a consequence, large areas of the Orange Free State and the Transvaal were laid to waste.

In conjunction with this, Kitchener authorized the use of internment camps to further isolate Boer fighters from their families, which would hopefully have the added effect of undermining the will to fight on the part of those whose families were now suffering the punitive effects of the war. The term "concentration camp" has fallen into disfavor in recent years for obvious reasons, and historians tend to prefer "internment camps" when describing the British camps, but the lingering effects of this experience still reside very much in the collective consciousness of the South African Afrikaans community.

**A camp near Cape Town**

The first two camps, situated in Pretoria and Bloemfontein, started as authentic refugee camps housing those displaced by the war for one reason or another, or for the families of Boer commando members who had surrendered. But once the scorched earth policy was rolled out, the families of active commando members were also driven into these camps, at which point they acquired the name "concentration camps."

It is also worth noting that a large number of blacks associated with Boer farms and homesteads were likewise interned under similarly restrictive conditions, but in separately located camps. Black families, whether or not they were actually associated with Boer families, were as deeply affected by the scorched earth policy as the other rural inhabitants of the Orange Free State and the Transvaal. According to some accounts, there was an ulterior motive on the part of the British in targeting black civilians in this manner, and this was to gain a source of captive or coerced labor for the various noncombatant roles necessary to support such a vast British expeditionary force. These roles not only included such necessary functions as wagon drivers, stockmen, herders and general camp labor, but also more specialized roles such as tracking and reconnaissance, for which they were often ideally suited. The British made widespread use of them, as did the Boer, albeit to a lesser degree.

After awhile, the use of camps, the scorched earth policy, and the extreme social hardships that all of this imposed upon the civilian population began to attract the attention of British liberals and humanitarians. A broadly conservative government was in power in Britain at the time, and the South African situation, now widely considered a social blight, provided the opposition Liberal party with partisan political ammunition. This was aided considerably by the work of one of the first and most influential British humanitarians and philanthropists of the age, a formidable woman by the name of Emily Hobhouse, who almost singlehandedly exposed and publicized the South African concentration camps.

**Hobhouse**

The British authorities in South Africa pursued a multi-tier system in the camps, insofar as ration distribution and general comforts within the wires were made available to a greater degree to the families of those men who voluntarily surrendered. Resources were withheld from the families of those men who did not. The result was widespread hunger and disease within the camps, and figures later produced suggest that some 4,177 women died, 22,074 children under the age of 16 died, and 1,676 non-combatant men died. It's estimated that the population in the camps numbered 85,000-94,000.

On June 18, 1901, Hobhouse produced a report following a tour of inspection of many such camps, entitled *To the S.A. Distress Fund, Report of a visit to the camps of women and children in the Cape and Orange River Colonies*. The damning nature of this report not only provoked measured concern in Parliament but also widespread revulsion among the wider Victorian British public, further consolidating a growing anti-war movement. There were many within the British establishment who began to ask whether the annihilation of the Boer and the absolute destruction of their lives and livelihoods could be considered a legitimate tactic of war.

Naturally, Kitchener came under increasing criticism, and his antipathy towards Emily Hobhouse caused him often to refer to her as "That Bloody Woman," a moniker that she apparently accepted with a great deal of pride and self-satisfaction.

In the meanwhile, she continued her public campaign, publishing and lecturing widely and collecting funds to improve conditions in the camps. To Lord Kitchener, she wrote, "I hope in future you will exercise greater width of judgement in the exercise of your high office. To carry out orders such as these is a degradation both to the office and the manhood of your soldiers. I feel ashamed to own you as a fellow-countryman."

In time, the British government was accused by both its opposition and members of its own party of pursuing a policy of extermination, and soon enough the question of human rights violations in South Africa became the opposition's clarion call. "When is a war not a war?" asked the Liberal Opposition Leader, Henry Campbell-Bannerman, to which he also answered, "When it is carried on by methods of barbarism in South Africa."

Against a backdrop of the explosive contents of Emily Hobhouse's report and the steady trickle of defamatory facts, the government found itself in a position requiring a response. This response took the form of a commission of inquiry, the Fawcett Commission. The Fawcett Commission was headed by a woman, Millicent Fawcett, a leader of the woman's suffrage movement who led an all-woman panel, making it quite unique for the time. Fawcett was a Liberal-Unionist, nominally a government insider, and the administration hoped for leniency in her report, but that was not to be the case. Fawcett submitted a report that went even further than Hobhouse in its unrestrained criticism of Kitchener's methods. As a result, responsibility for the administration of the camps was handed over to the civilian authorities, philanthropic organizations were given access, and conditions steadily began to improve.

**Fawcett**

It was broadly concluded that Kitchener had not pursued a deliberate policy of extermination, but simply that the scale of camp administration, and the level of priority the camps occupied in the overall military equation, inevitably resulted in unacceptable neglect. Kitchener was a soldier, not a civilian administrator, and the deployment and use of a system of camps to accommodate those who were accumulated there as a byproduct of a unique war was simply too new.

Other commentators and subsequent historians have been less charitable. Kitchener, they argue, used the deplorable conditions and the suffering of the inmates as propaganda. Word of what was taking place would inevitably leak to the front lines, and naturally, it would add incentive to many Boer men sitting on the fence to surrender. When no longer able to practically do this, Kitchener changed tack, ordering that his forces in the field not bring in women and children for internment but send them across the lines to join the fighting men. Thus encumbered, the commandos would find it increasingly difficult to survive, let alone maneuver, and once more, surrenders would be encouraged.

On the battlefield, Kitchener was no less diligent in applying his revised military policy. Roberts had begun a program of fortifying strategic bridges, railway junctions, and other places of importance against Boer attacks, and Kitchener began to expand on this program with the construction of blockhouses. These were in essence strong-points located in a grid system across the great expanses, linked by barbed wire. They eventually numbered 8,000 and were manned by a garrison of 60,000 soldiers and supported by 25,000 non-white auxiliaries. The blockhouse system was probably only useful in combination with the mass drives that Kitchener also implemented, but as an obstruction to free Boer movement across the landscape, they were certainly of at least some value. The drives were mass infantry movements mounted to keep the Boer mobile, and where possible to trap them against blockhouses and large garrison forces. This was feasible in the open country of the Orange Free State, and although some success was recorded, on the whole, against the mobility of the Boer commandos, it was not all that impactful. To patrol railway lines, which were always vulnerable, armored trains were deployed, but again, they were too few and too cumbersome to really have any widespread effect.

While no one policy was terribly successful on its own, all of these policies succeeded in wearing down Boer resistance, and by the beginning of 1902, a combination of dwindling numbers, hunger, diminishing supplies, and a general sense of hopelessness had begun to erode Boer morale. By April 1902, there were approximately 21,000 Boer combatants left active in the field, many without horses, rifles, or ammunition. British forces in South Africa numbered 240,000 at the peak of deployment, with huge numbers of auxiliaries. It was beginning to become clear to Boer leadership that the struggle could not continue for much longer, and at the very least, some kind of a negotiated peace would be preferable to their annihilation.

By April 1902, Kitchener was at his wit's end over the entire conflict, and he was anxious to see it end. Under safe conduct, he allowed the Boer leadership to meet in the town of Klerksdorp on the border of the Transvaal and the Orange River Colony. Attending this meeting, among others, were Transvaal President Schalk Burger, Transvaal military commander Botha, General Koos de la Rey, and Orange Free State President Martinus Steyn. General de Wet and General Hertzog were also in attendance. The Transvaalers tended to be more open to considering peace negotiations, while the Orange Free Staters, on the whole, took a more trenchant position, arguing for a continuation of the war. A more pragmatic presence was General Smuts, who, although not ranked among the top tier of Boer leadership, was present because of his legal training and his clear understanding of British diplomatic process.

Prominent on the British side was Alfred Milner, an extremely influential character in British South Africa and one of the original architects of the war. By 1902, the geopolitical balance was moving towards a confrontation of some sort between the two major power blocs of Europe, and Milner was looking at the world in this context. The British Empire had reached the apex of its geographic scope, and the question was now less one of continued global expansion than the consolidation of the British Empire into a form that would not only accommodate the growing mood of independence among such overseas dominions as Canada, Australia, New Zealand and India, but one that would maintain such cohesion in the face of widespread war. South Africa was the only substantive British overseas territory that was home to a white European population that did not identify fundamentally as British. The smaller African territories, and such similar territories elsewhere, were British colonies and not British dominions, and their native populations did not at that point warrant consideration as independent entities. The Boer could not be classified that way.

**Milner**

These considerations compelled Milner to seek a permanent British dominance in South Africa, in order that South Africa as a future British dominion would stand alongside the other major pillars of the empire when push came to shove. In part, his strategy to achieve this was to encourage the inflow of British capital for reconstruction, the mass immigration of British labor to facilitate industry and mining, and the imposition of the English language as the language of government, the judiciary, and education. In the face of all of this, the petty anxieties of a minor race seeking to preserve their identity counted as very little.

Thus, when the Boer committee returned its position on peace, marking as its minimum negotiating position the retention of independent Boer rule over the republics, Milner dismissed this outright. Unconditional surrender was his minimum negotiating position, and he would not be moved.

Kitchener now had to become something of a diplomat. He took aside the more moderate Boer leaders, like Botha and Smuts, and expressed his opinion that under the current conservative establishment in Britain, concessions of that magnitude would be impossible. A brutal and costly war had been fought and funded by the British for the purpose of adding South Africa to the British sphere of influence, and that, at the very least, was what was expected. However, he reminded the Boer that an election in Britain was imminent, and the likelihood would be that a Liberal government would follow. Given the Liberal position over such issues as the internment camps and other harsh realities of the war, the Boer should wait for the elections to begin sounding the British government out for a more equitable distribution of power and resource.

Smuts, of course, recognized this immediately. His history, his training, and his past engagement with the British softened his view, and naturally, he was better placed than his more bucolic comrades to recognize that the independence of a small race in a larger, imperial world was temporarily impractical. He did not like it, but he realized that it was unavoidable, at least in the short term. On his side stood Botha, now a very influential figure among the Boer, and it was with this fundamental realization that the two men guided the Boer establishment on the next step towards a negotiated peace.

On May 15, 1902, a grand council of Boer leaders gathered under an expansive marquee in the market town of Vereeniging, 40 miles southeast of Johannesburg, and here the final Boer position would be established. A series of difficult and acrimonious discussions took place, with moderates led by Smuts and Botha grappling against hardliners led by de Wet and Hertzog. There remained a strong Boer army in the field, and the war could easily be continued for a season or two, as the hardliners pointed out, but what, ultimately, would be the result of this? Terms of surrender could, under current circumstances, be negotiated that would salvage the Boer language, customs and national ideals. In the event of an unconditional surrender, all of that would be lost. Instead, the Boer would indeed be a subject people of the British crown, but they could retain their identity as a separate people and could live to fight a different kind of war on another day.[7]

On May 17, 1902, Smuts, Botha, and Hertzog were sent to negotiate with Milner. Negotiations were rancorous and painful, but in the end, in exchange for their survival, the Boer leadership accepted the loss of their independence and an acknowledgement of British sovereignty over the

---

[7] A point worth noting is that Smuts negotiated a key clause in the agreement that limited any black involvement in future government. Part of the British stated reason for entering the war was the disparity in rights available to whites, Indians and blacks in the Transvaal, and certain promises were made to grant greater inclusion to blacks and Indians upon an eventual British victory. Milner had argued that non-white voting rights would be implemented upon a grant of self-government. Smuts had altered that terminology to read that non-white voting rights would be considered upon a grant of self-government, which effectively pushed back that possibility until such time as the white minority accepted it, which in the event never occurred.

republics. At the same time, extremely generous reconstruction funding was authorized, which Milner distributed quickly, dramatically easing the conditions of a great many impoverished Boer.

Moreover, the treaty, known thereafter as the Treaty of Vereeniging, left open the possibility of self-government under the terms of British dominion. This provision was vague, and its terms were unspecified, but it held promise for the future, and for the time being, that was enough.

**Amanda Calitz's picture of the table on which the treaty was signed**

**The Union of South Africa**

The events that followed the Boer War and the treaty quickly brought about the creation of modern South Africa. The two new colonies of the Orange River and the Transvaal were incorporated into the British Empire, under military rule initially and then under formal British administration, with Milner serving as de facto governor-general of South Africa. He implemented his policy of promoting British capital and immigration vigorously, with mixed results.

Initially, the old Boer leadership, with Botha and Smuts now somewhat leading the pack, retreated into the background and refused any kind of engagement with the colonial government on any level. Milner did try to draw prominent Boer leaders into the various new colonial administrations, but this was almost always unsuccessful. No Boer leader would formally associate with the British government, which left Milner entirely accountable for the results of his policies.

Milner was confronted by the need to restart the Transvaal mining industry in order to jumpstart the economy. British capital was available to achieve this, but British labor was slow to avail itself of the opportunity. Black labor at that point was not sufficiently developed to fill the gap, so Milner was forced to contemplate imported Chinese indentured labor. This proved so universally unpopular, both in South Africa and in Britain, that it brought down the British government and discredited Milner and his entire pro-British policy in South Africa.

This was precisely the moment that Kitchener had predicted, and a Liberal victory in the 1906 British general election offered the opportunity for General Smuts to open negotiations. A strong personal sympathy and friendship developed between Smuts, who was a man of towering intellect and great statesmanship, and the new British Prime Minister, Henry Campbell-Bannerman. Smuts' position was simply that Britain would be wise to cultivate the friendship of the Boer since it would be they who would ultimately decide the direction in which South Africa would tilt when the time came for taking sides in a global war. Campbell-Bannerman agreed, and the broad terms for the self-government of the colonies were established.

**Campbell-Bannerman**

Self-government within the British Empire implied a domestically elected legislature, prime minister, and cabinet, under the broad and very loose terms of British superintendentship. This was the status of all the substantive British overseas dominions at that time, and it was seen in South Africa as an obvious precursor to South African dominion status within the Commonwealth. An election was held in 1907, and in the Orange River Colony, Abraham Fischer became the first (and only) prime minister. In Transvaal, Botha was similarly elected, with Smuts as his deputy.

**Fischer**

The next constitutional development was the amalgamation of all four British territories in South Africa into a single unified colony. Again, it was Smuts who led the process, which was largely one of reconciling the various peculiarities and race policies of each colony into a single constitutional format. The Cape, for example, enjoyed a long tradition of free franchise and liberal race policies, while the Transvaal remained deeply conservative and antagonistic towards any non-white inclusion in government or the administration. The British, on the whole, were amicable to South African unity, but they were forced by circumstance and political reality to swallow an overall race policy that was extremely retrogressive when compared to contemporary British thinking.

Nonetheless, the Union of South Africa was formalized by Parliament on September 20, 1909, and it came into being on May 31, 1910.

In both former colonies, the question of race was deliberately kept off the agenda as the election campaigns went ahead. The British were willing to ignore the obvious anomaly of a whites-only electorate in a multi-racial colony, but only in the interests of peace and harmony in the region. The issue, therefore, was best ignored and left to be dealt with at a later date. In the matter of race relations, the Orange Free State, under the sway of a deeply conservative and right-wing establishment, would tolerate no discussion whatsoever of black political engagement. The electorate of the Transvaal remained almost exclusively white, with only a minimum of Indian participation, with Natal retaining its constitution that barred Indian participation and limited black involvement to almost zero. The Cape, on the other hand, held on to its colorblind franchise but found itself swimming very much against the tide as its northern neighbors entrenched an attitude of formal racial exclusion.

Black political activity, however, was beginning to gather momentum. In the Cape, it existed at an advanced stage, with several black language newspapers, numerous high profile and active political figures, and several organizations falling just short of political parties. There were also numerous independent churches that functioned in an extremely political environment, and, in fact, it was in this environment that the radical black nationalist movement began to push out its first shoots.

The most politically active region of the country was the Witwatersrand, where by 1910 black laborers from all across the region met and mingled. Most of the Chinese had by then been sent home, replaced almost entirely by blacks. Migrant labor in the South African gold mines was drawn from a very wide catchment, with Congolese mingling with southern Sotho, and Nyasas sharing a common lingua franca with Mozambicans and Northern Rhodesians.[8] Revolutionary ideas easily followed these arteries of migrant labor, and as men entered and assimilated the cash economy, so they grew fluent in modern life and politics. As a consequence, the mine compounds of the Witwatersrand were hotbeds of nationalist political activity and the free exchange of ideas.

It was in this environment that radical political ideologies were developed and organizations were founded. In 1882, the Ethiopian Church had been created in Pretoria, with its rallying cry being Psalm 68:31: "Ethiopia shall soon stretch forth its hands unto God." This psalm was interpreted to mean that God and the black races would soon link hands in the common purpose of liberating the nation and all the subject people of the world. This was a powerful concept, and it produced an ecumenical movement that was more politics than religion that established the first organized black forum with a mass following. Toward the end of the 19th century, the Ethiopian Church allied with the African Methodist Episcopal Church, or the AME, in the United States, creating a powerful movement. The AME, indeed, would emerge as the largest black church in South Africa, as it remains today. Interestingly, it was recognized in the Transvaal, but it was banned in Natal and gained no particular foothold in the Cape.

---

[8] The lingua franca that developed on the mines was known as 'Fanagolo,' containing elements of English, Dutch, and numerous native languages. Being able to speak it lent young blacks the impression that they could speak English and whites that they could speak a native language. In practical terms, it was both and neither.

Even as the union of South Africa was coming together, its various leaders recognized the regional differences, especially when it came to interactions with black residents. Smuts spoke not only for the political establishment of the Transvaal but for the left wing of the Afrikaner movement as a whole, while Hertzog stood proxy as the spokesman for the conservative wing. Representing Natal was Prime Minister Frederick Robert Moor, and speaking on behalf of the Cape was Prime Minister John Merriman. Another vocal and passionate representative of the Cape was liberal Afrikaner parliamentarian William Schreiner, the younger brother of the feminist author Olive Schreiner.

William Schreiner was in many respects years ahead of his time. He wrote to Smuts in the days prior to the convening of the conference that brought about the union, imploring him to guide the conference in the direction of fairness and justice. He asked whether the liberal Cape tradition alone would be robust enough to stand up to the interests of three territorial partners that were hostile to it: "The freedom to which all men are born in a free land is as true as their alleged equality is false … But,' he argued, 'their freedom cannot be real if they do not have full opportunity to achieve equality."

John Merriman, the Cape Prime Minister, argued for a Cape-style franchise, the qualification for which would be high enough to attract "civilized" blacks. It was argued in reply that this would simply deny the vote to poor whites, an entire generation of which was created by the Anglo-Boer War. Merriman's comments on this are interesting, because he did not necessarily like the Cape electoral system, but he regarded it as a useful pressure valve. Although "noisy and evil-smelling," it was nonetheless the safest contingency to prevent further fighting.

Smuts' opinions were varied and often contradictory, all of which, as his biographers have noted, tended to reveal an unresolved view of the issue. As an academic, he was quite often apt to lapse into hazy theoretics, using the language of paleoanthropology and evolutionary divergence. At other times, he suggested that the issue be left for wiser minds of the future to resolve. In this regard, he was referring not so much to himself, but to his constituents, who remained perplexed at the very suggestion that the natives in the countryside had any conception of modern politics. An extract from a letter written by Smuts to the British economist and social scientist John A. Hobson contained this remark: "My impression is that the only sound policy at this stage is to avoid any attempt at a comprehensive solution of the various questions surrounding the political status and rights of the native. With the chaotic state in which public opinion on this subject is at present, any solution would be a poor compromise which might probably prejudice a fairer and more statesmanlike settlement later on."

There was some truth in that, but ultimately it was his view that the natives of Africa resided in the kindergarten of life, and that it fell upon the white man to guide them forth toward the light of civilization by increments until that day in the far distant future when they might be allowed some small share of their own destiny. It was not so much a question of should the black man be granted a political voice, but whether it was in his own best interests to have such a voice at all. Needless to say, 21st century readers recognize the racism and paternalism in it, but in the early 20th century, Smuts' contemporaries would hardly bat an eye at such a thought.

It might be interesting to include Gandhi's view of all of this, for he was very much an interested observer of a process that involved not a single non-white member. He said, "Civilization is gradually making headway among the Negroes. Pious missionaries deliver to them the message of Christ as they have understood it, open schools for them, and teach them how to read and write, but many whom, being illiterate and therefore strangers to civilization, were so far free from many vices, have now become corrupt." The essence of this message was repeated often, and in many forms by a man fighting a race war in South Africa who was speculating whether all races were created equal. Gandhi's campaign in South Africa was categorically not waged with any view of black advancement in mind - his interest was narrowly focused on the plight of Indians, and if Indians could not be granted full equality with whites in South Africa, then at least let them not be legislated for alongside blacks or lumped in with blacks indiscriminately as "non-white." As he also put it, "Ours is one continual struggle against a degradation sought to be inflicted upon us by the Europeans, who desire to degrade us to the level of the raw Kaffir whose occupation is hunting, and whose sole ambition is to collect a certain number of cattle to buy a wife with, and then, pass his life in indolence and nakedness."

The antipathy implicit in this comment between Indians and blacks was no less a fact of life than any other in the complex race equation of South Africa. The main point of contact between blacks and whites in the country was in the labor market, which, in a way, was unfortunate, because at that point the least qualified members of each side to approach and judge one another were pushed together. Most whites only knew black people who labored in their home, but Gandhi did not even have that. He employed no black servants, labored alongside no black person, and sought no contact or alliance with the black political establishment. He mingled entirely with whites and Indians and concluded in the end that that struggle he was engaged in was an Indian struggle, not an African one. As such, he ultimately determined it would best be fought in India.

In the end, the conundrum that Smuts and other white political colleagues faced was one they decided was too complex and multi-faceted to be dealt with in a convention meant to forge a consensus. Thus, it was agreed that each region would retain within a proposed union its pre-existing constitution, espousing whatever practices each preferred.

In the end, Jan Smuts would be proved wrong, for the wiser heads were not those in the future, but those in the past. The earliest European activity in the Cape was undertaken with the cooperation and involvement of all citizens in mind, and that remained the preferred vision of many older liberals. As it turned out, the younger generation took a harder line. Each time the black political elite knocked on the door, the door was bolted a little tighter, until, as the National

Convention wound up, it became clear that the door would never willingly be opened.

For the time being, the British observed these events from afar and did not seek to subvert the wishes of the people on the ground. Again, this was an example of political expediency overriding the moral requirements. There could be no doubt that the situation did not bode well in the long term, but in the short term, the British Empire was arming to deal with a more clear and present danger than blacks in South Africa. Smuts noted as much: "The war between the white races will run its course, and pass away and may, if followed by a statesman-like settlement, one day only be remembered as a great thunderstorm, which purified the atmosphere of the sub-continent. But the native question will never pass away. It will get more difficult as time goes on, and the day may come when the evils and horrors of this war will appear as nothing in comparison with its after-effects produced on the native mind."

Indeed, a few years later, South Africa would be playing an important role in World War I. At the outbreak of war, Britain lacked the necessary organization and manpower to deal with the occupation of German South West Africa and German East Africa, so this task was assigned to South Africa, which would have to rely on its own resources. Almost at the moment that this understanding was reached, however, a rebellion broke out in the ranks of the Union Defense Force, and a significant number of anti-British South African troops attempted to cross into German South West Africa in order to declare for the Germans. It must be remembered that Germany had been the closest thing to a foreign alliance that the old republics had ever enjoyed, and a great many Afrikaans speaking servicemen did not see the Germans as the enemy. Furthermore, they recognized an opportunity to overthrow British rule in South Africa now that the British Empire was engaged in a European war.

Ultimately, Smuts, as Minister of Defense, crushed the rebellion, and he guided South Africa into World War I as a loyal member of the British alliance. This would also be the case in World War II, but that conflict would bring about the advent of the South African republic, and the descent of South Africa into its darkest phase of statutory racism and apartheid.

## World War I

At the outbreak of war in August 1914, the Union of South Africa was just four years old and the greatest challenge to the cohesion of the British Empire lay before it. By then, the character of the British Empire had evolved, and the principal territories were no longer as closely allied to the center as they had once been. Increasingly, the empire was being referred to as a "Commonwealth," with each territory allied to the Crown but enjoying nominal independence. India remained under direct rule, and although a certain amount of diplomatic maneuvering was required, India's entry into the war on the Allied side was never really in doubt.[9] A vague

---

[9] The Indian nationalist/independence movement was fully formed by then, and agitation of Indian dominion status was well underway.

commitment to consider dominion status in the aftermath of the war mollified the growing Indian nationalist movement, while Australia and New Zealand were increasingly part of the Asian security equation, which involved concerns about the potential of Japanese imperial ambitions, and Canada was now much more engaged with the United States in terms of trade and security. With a significant French language demographic, there was never any certainty of Canada's commitment to Crown in a time of war. Ultimately, the populations of these dominions quickly threw their lot in with the British after little debate, and contingents of men immediately began to flood into Europe and the Middle East from the colonies, making it a true world war.

In South Africa, however, the situation was far less certain. South Africa was a British dominion, but its collective loyalty to the British Crown was very much in doubt. A little over a decade earlier, one of the most bitter imperial wars on record had been fought between the two white races of South Africa, and the notion of reconciliation so soon afterward, to the extent that South Africa would willingly go to war for Britain, was untested to say the least. During the Boer War, the Boer had fought with Mauser rifles and Krupp artillery, and the German Empire was as close to a foreign relation as the Boer republics had. Thus, while a significant number of South African servicemen did not acknowledge either the British as an ally or the Germans as an enemy, the expectation that they fight on those terms was sure to open up wounds that had barely begun to heal. Indeed, there was a strong movement among the hardline Afrikaner faction which nurtured a hope that, with the British fully preoccupied with war in Europe, an opportunity might be there to evict them from South Africa altogether and reestablish the republic.

Of course, the British faced difficult and more immediate dilemma in Europe. The British establishment entirely appreciated the agony of indecision that collectively afflicted the whites of South Africa, with one side fanatically loyal and the other grimly unreconciled, but the war needed to be fought and South Africa was the only British dominion in the southern African region capable of dealing with the German presence there. The Cape and the naval base at Simonstown remained of supreme importance to the Allied Powers, as did the British deep-water port of Walvis Bay, which was little more than an enclave surrounded on all sides by German South West Africa. Besides that, an important radio relay station was located in German South West Africa, and that territory clearly presented a risk to British sovereignty in South Africa. Put simply, it needed to go.

Further afield, the situation was no less complicated. The territory of German East Africa, the future Tanganyika, was home to several deep-water ports, most importantly Dar-es-Salaam, which was also able to host heavy naval shipping and submarines. That presented a significant risk to Allied naval and merchant shipping in both the Indian Ocean and Atlantic Ocean. Bearing in mind the roles of India, Australia, and New Zealand in the war effort, and the vulnerability of the Suez Canal, it was seen as vital to establish full Allied control over all the main African ports in the south and east.

While these war aims were obvious, it was also obvious that dealing with the German threat in the east and south would require a significant military undertaking, and at that early stage in the war, with neither the organization or the manpower to attend to it, the British relied on South Africans. Soon after the declaration of war, a formal request was submitted to South Africa to annex German South West Africa with its own resources. This was obviously a major request and a significant responsibility, but General Botha and General Smuts agreed without hesitation. Smuts' appreciation of the British was not without reservations, but both men recognized that if South Africa did not firmly and resolutely hitch its wagon to the British side, then it would most certainly be left behind and would never realize its full potential as a member of the first tier of global nations.

While this reality was also acknowledged by many others, it was rejected by the vast majority of Afrikaans-speaking South Africans. By then, the difficulties of race and ideology in the Union of South Africa had already manifested themselves in a series of bitter and violent labor disputes, centered on the Witwatersrand but affecting industry throughout the Union. The causes of the various strikes and lockouts were general, but underscoring this industrial action was the steady rise of Afrikaner nationalism and a determination to protect white, Afrikaans-speaking workers against unfair competition from lower-paid blacks. Much of the anger expressed was directed at the government (Smuts and Botha in particular), and as World War I began, the stability of the government and the feasibility of a British dominion hung very much in the balance. Smuts and Botha were seen by a majority of their colleagues and compatriots as having sold out to the British, and the decision of the government to honor the British request to mount a campaign against the Germans in South West Africa was seen as clear evidence of this.

Despite internal opposition, both Botha and Smuts were determined to carry it through. In part, this was to establish the principle of South African loyalty to the British Crown, but also to prove that the Union of South Africa was viable and a regional superpower. Furthermore, while a South African campaign to annex South West Africa would, in theory, add the territory to the dominions of the Crown, in practical terms, it would add territory to South Africa.

Smuts, as Minister of Defense, had the responsibility for creating the Union Defence Force, or UDF. This proved to be a delicate, political balancing act, which required fair Boer representation at a command level, but at the same time established an armed force that would be both stable and obedient to the civilian government. To command the UDF, Smuts appointed Brigadier-General Christian Beyers, the highly respected and senior Boer War commander. Beyers' loyalty, however, was first and foremost to the Afrikaner nation, and not necessarily to the government. Although he remained loyal to both Botha and Smuts as fellow members of the Afrikaner nation and as comrades in arms, he was not a supporter of the pro-British position of the government.

In fact, Beyers was bitterly opposed to South African participation in the war, and in this regard, he was backed up by some very powerful voices. The aging General Jacobus de la Rey was one of these. He stood firmly against South African participation in the war, and what he had to say about it was taken seriously in many quarters. On September 15, 1914, Beyers resigned his commission, writing, "It is sad that the war is being waged against the 'barbarism' of the Germans. We have forgiven but not forgotten all the barbarities committed in our own country during the South African War."[10]

Meanwhile, stationed in the Northern Cape, along the frontier with German South West Africa, was a force of about six-hundred 600 UDF members under the command of General Salomon "Manie" Maritz. Maritz was a "bitter-ender," which in South African parlance meant one who advocated a fight to end rather than surrender at the end of the Boer War. In mid-September 1914, in the midst of preparations to mount the South West Africa Campaign, Maritz led his commandos across the Orange River and into South West Africa and declared for the Germans. He also declared a provisional government and announced the removal of the Union of South Africa from the British Empire.

GENERAAL MANIE MARITZ.

---

[10] Beyers was referring to the use of concentration camps to isolate Boer women and children from the fighting men, to starve out the latter. Thousands of Boer women and children died in these camps.

# Maritz

Smuts had certainly been expecting something along these lines, and he seized the opportunity when it came to stamping the authority of the government on the rebellious armed forces. Martial law was declared, and the "Maritz Rebellion" was systematically crushed. A commando unit under the command of Beyers was also attacked and destroyed. With what can only be described as extreme prejudice, Smuts acted swiftly and decisively to bring the matter to a conclusion. In the end, he was able to retain the loyalty of the armed forces, which, albeit reluctantly and with deep reservations, held firmly to the policy of war on behalf of the Allied Powers.

When the dust settled, it was quietly acknowledged that the loyalty of the UDF hung on a knife's edge, and for a while South Africa teetered on the very brink of civil war. However, now that it was over, Smuts was at last in a position to plan the South West Africa Campaign, and he set about doing this immediately.

South Africa conducted two major military campaigns during the war, known as the German South West Africa Campaign and the German East Africa Campaign. The former was fought between September 1914 and July 1915, and it marked the coming of age of Smuts as a military genius, which was surprising because he had no formal military training at all. He entered service during the Boer War after the collapse of the republics, at which point the guerrilla phase of the war had already started. Prior to that, he held the position of State Attorney of the Transvaal and had never fired a shot in anger. In fact, many anecdotal reports say that he never did, conducting numerous successful operations and campaigns without ever personally resorting to gunfire. His brilliance was in tactical assault and evasion, and a wider strategic appreciation of waging war. He was awarded the rank of general in the informal manner of the Boer commandos, and he retained that rank for the remainder of his life as a mark of respect.

The German South West Africa Campaign was the first chapter of mechanized desert warfare in the annals of military history, and it remains the essential template for similar wars and campaigns. Upon analysis, however, it was more of a feat of logistics and military engineering than military maneuver, which would often be the case in desert warfare. The Germans did not defend the colony with a great deal of commitment, resting on the assumption that they would achieve victory in Europe and then get back any lost colonies elsewhere across the world. Early in the war, that was a fair position to take since the odds of a German victory were good, so the strategy in Africa was simply to tie up as much Allied manpower as possible in a wild goose chase from one end of the colony to another, offering surrender only when run to ground.

The broad strategy of the South West Africa Campaign was a vast double envelopment. Two armies were deployed, one commanded by General Botha and the other by General Smuts, landing respectively at Walvis Bay and Swakopmund and attempting to trap the defending garrison in a giant pincer. The strategy was simple enough and sound, and its success can be attributed almost entirely to the vast logistical feats of fielding an army, supplying it under punishing conditions, and providing wells and roads and railway lines upon which it could move forward. The Germans remained one step ahead until they could no longer do so, and they then surrendered in good grace. As far as World War I campaigns went, this one was remarkably bloodless, with the South Africans losing 185 killed (most in non-combatant circumstances) and the Germans just over 100. The territory was placed under a military government for the duration of the war, leaving General Smuts to turn his attention to German East Africa.

Ideally, the British wanted General Botha to command and lead the Allied forces in the German East Africa Campaign, but the war remained so deeply unpopular in South Africa, so it was decided that he would remain in South Africa and run the government. A British officer, General Sir Horace Smith-Dorrien, was instead appointed by the War Office to take command of the East Africa Campaign, but en route to South Africa, he fell ill and was unable to take up his command. After much consideration, the job was given to Smuts.

The difficulty in this regard was that Smuts was not a member of the British Army, nor any army for that matter, and he had never undergone any sort of formal military training. This time, he would be commanding a British and Commonwealth force, so it was necessary for him to hold a British Army commission. He was therefore quietly inducted into the British Army as an honorary member with the rank Lieutenant General, which, at 47, made him the youngest man to date to be awarded that rank.

East Africa was divided between the British and German empires along the broadly speaking line of the modern frontier between Kenya and Tanzania. By international treaty, it was understood that the colonial possessions of each empire would not prosecute the war, maintaining neutrality for the sake of not exciting the natives.[11] Both colonial governors were committed to honoring this convention, but the German military attaché in East Africa, Colonel Paul Emile von Lettow-Vorbeck, had other ideas. His objective, not unlike that of the German commanders in South West Africa, was to force the commitment of as much Allied manpower as possible into a largely irrelevant theater simply to ease pressure against German forces on the Western Front. By then, the certainty of a German victory in Europe was not quite so keenly felt, and the strategy was to avoid a general defeat.

Initially, von Lettow-Vorbeck commanded the battlefield. The British territory (Kenya and Uganda) was only protected by a weak, colonial militia, a handful of imperial troops, and a few battalions of the King's African Rifles. Inevitably, with a weight of naval superiority, the British were able to blockade the coast and main ports of German East Africa, which included sinking the German warship SMS *Königsberg* in a daring operation, but they lacked the resources to dislodge the Germans from the interior in and around Mount Kilimanjaro. From that stronghold, using the local *Schutztruppe*, or native troops under German command, von-Lettow-Vorbeck conducted a campaign of attrition into British territory. He repeatedly targeted the Uganda

---

[11] This was the Main Act of the Berlin Conference of 1884/5

Railway, which ran parallel to the international frontier.[12]

Smuts arrived in the theater in February 1916 at the head of a large South African force. Now energized, the British turned the tide of the campaign, after which von-Lettow-Vorbeck adopted the strategy of a fighting retreat, leading the Allied forces in a mobile operation that continued until a few weeks after the signing of the Armistice in November 1918.[13] The Allied victory, such as it was, represented another feat of logistics as von Lettow-Vorbeck, leading a largely native army, ranged across the East African interior. Troops from India, several parts of British Africa, as well as Rhodesia and South Africa were employed in the theater, along with hundreds of thousands of native carriers and porters. In the end, the East Africa Campaign degenerated into a battle more against the conditions of tropical warfare than enemy action, with several times the casualties recorded from disease than from contact with the enemy. Neither side could definitively claim victory or defeat, and in the end, von Lettow-Vorbeck and Smuts acknowledged one another's brilliance. They later became friends.

At the beginning of 1917, Smuts was recalled from East Africa to London, ostensibly to represent South Africa at the Imperial Conference of that year, but more practically to enter the British high command as an appointed member of British Prime Minister David Lloyd George's War Cabinet. By then, with the entry of the United States into the war, an Allied victory was looking likely, and Smuts was required at general HQ. His political genius, no less highly regarded than his military, was then applied to questions as diverse as Palestine and Home Rule in Ireland, and later to help craft the terms of peace that would be imposed on the defeated Central Powers. Smuts, incidentally, was among those who regarded the terms of the Treaty of Versailles as too harsh and initially refused to sign it on behalf of South Africa, but he was eventually persuaded to do so by Botha.

Perhaps Smuts' greatest contribution during this period was as a founding architect of the League of Nations. As an Allied victory approached, one of the most challenging questions became how to replace the authority of the four empires that collapsed as a consequence of the war. With the Germans, Russians, Ottomans, and Austrians all losing their empires, the question was how to manage the many territories liberated from these empires, especially since so few of them had any past as independent states. President Woodrow Wilson was the first to moot the concept of a world government named the League of Nations, but it was Smuts more than any other who applied his mind to the practical formation of such an organization. It was he who designed and established the many institutions and organizations necessary to found and practically manage such a groundbreaking international association, which was further confirmation of his prodigious capability and his standing among international statesmen. The

---

[12] The *Schutztruppe*, or colonial protection force, comprised battalions of native troops, or 'askari', commanded by metropolitan German officers. Von Lettow-Vorbeck went on a recruitment drive early in the war, and at its peak, he commanded a force of about 20,000 men at arms, with many more in auxiliary roles.

[13] The East African Campaign of WWI is regarded as the longest running campaign of WWI. It began at the moment of the declaration and ended only after the signing of the Armistice. Von Lettow-Vorbeck offered his surrender but did not acknowledge defeat.

League of Nations would ultimately fail and disband, but as the forerunner of the United Nations, the essence of its mission was to replace global empires with global government.

Of particular interest to South Africa at this point were those territories that it had liberated from the Germans during the war. It was decided that a system of governing mandates be put in place to be divided up among the victorious powers. The Middle East, for example, was divided up between the French and the British, but it was South Africa that was given an exclusive mandate over the territory of South West Africa. This, on the surface at least, was part of the British mandate, but in truth, it was a reward to South Africa for the conquest of the territory.

Smuts regarded this as entirely just, but he was aggrieved somewhat when South Africa was not given East Africa in respect of the dominant South African role in that campaign. There was, by then, already a degree of wariness in Whitehall over the apparent micro-imperialist ambitions of South Africa, and while handing over South West Africa, 95% percent of which was desert, was one thing, East Africa was another altogether. The Tanganyika territory thus became a British mandate, which, incidentally, finally created the reality for Cecil John Rhodes' Cape-Cairo vision.[14]

The South African mandate over South West Africa would evolve into de facto South African annexation, after which successive South African governments tended to regard the territory as a fifth province of South Africa. Under the terms of its mandate, the territory remained under the control of the League of Nations, and then the United Nations, but South Africa's refusal to relinquish control of the region when requested to do so would subsequently set the tone for later confrontations between South Africa and the international community.

### The Emergence of Black Politics in South Africa

On January 8, 1912, the iconic South African indigenous political party, the African National Congress (ANC), was founded. This was the culmination of years of organization and political development. The National Conference, discussed above, defined the terms under which the four colonies would be federated into the Union of South Africa, but any mechanism for the inclusion of the black majority in the political process of a future dominion was conspicuously absent. The British government accepted this state of affairs, passing the South Africa Act of 1910 with almost no query in regard to this glaring exclusion. The requirements of imperial unity in the face of an inevitable European war overrode the essential principals of the British Empire, and the matter was quietly swept under the rug.

In the aftermath of the National Conference, William Schreiner organized a shadow conference in the black township of Waaihoek outside Bloemfontein. The conference was intended to be a forum within which a general black response to the National Convention would be formulated.

---

[14] The relevant British territories included South Africa, Bechuanaland, Southern Rhodesia, Northern Rhodesia, Nyasaland, Tanganyika, Kenya, Sudan, and Egypt. Each was a British dependent territory or a British protectorate.

This was styled the South African Native Convention (SANC), and much of the conference was dominated by an address given by the member for native affairs in the Orange River parliament.

**Schreiner**

The Reverend Dewdney Drew, who was noted for his pro-African sympathies, was invited to speak at the conference, and he did. While acknowledging that the Union Bill fell far short of "equal rights for all civilized men," Drew was also inclined to adopt a cautionary tone.[15] He advised acceptance of the broad terms of the document in the belief that any agitation against it would simply stir the embers of white paranoia, inviting an even deeper assault against the rights and liberties of blacks. There was space within the proposed constitution for black participation on a local level, including qualified franchise in the Cape, so it seemed to him wiser to prove political maturity before demanding greater representation.

Although this message was discouraging, there was certainly a great deal of sense in it, and it was probably a fair assessment of the lay of the land. The Union Bill, however, required passage through the British House of Commons and royal assent, and toward the end of 1909, all the various prime ministers and interested parties set off for London to bear witness to the adoption

---

[15] 'Equal rights for all civilized men' was one of Cecil Rhodes' many mantras.

of the South Africa Act. A 9-man delegation of black representatives was assembled and led by William Schreiner to travel to London to approach the British Government with black South African concerns. Gandhi also traveled to London at the head of a delegation of South African Indians to present the Indian case in respect of South African union, but he rejected Schreiner's appeal that the two delegations combine forces.

During the event, the native delegation was entertained and heard by members of the government, the opposition, and the liberal establishment, but in the end they were made to understand that no changes to the essential character of the draft bill would be entertained. John Tengo Jabavu, a leading Cape political figure, newspaper editor, and writer, addressed a farewell breakfast hosted by the Aboriginal Protection Society. During this, he remarked that just a decade earlier, he had been invited by the Afrikaner Bond, the Dutch-speaking political party in the Cape, to stand as a candidate in the Cape Parliament. Now, under the terms of the draft act, no such thing would be possible. This hardly represented progress, and from where he was standing, it was an assault by one section of the population against another. The address concluded with the rueful observation that a parting of the ways between black and white in South Africa had finally come to pass.

While this was certainly the case, it's only fair to note that John Merriman, Prime Minister of the Cape Colony, argued vehemently for the extension of the Cape qualified franchise to the rest of the Union, but ultimately he was unsuccessfully. The Cape qualified franchise remained in effect and black representation in local forums was encouraged, but nothing of the sort was to be entertained in the federal parliament, which would be exclusively white.

Meanwhile, the South African Native Convention continued to exist as a political organization, acting as a voice against discriminatory legislation until it was agreed that a permanent organization was required, which led the way to establishment of the South African National Native Congress, the forerunner of the iconic African National Congress. The principal founders were Saul Msane, Josiah Gumede, John Dube, Pixley ka Isaka Seme, and Sol Plaatje, collectively representing the acme of the South African native political movement.

Perhaps the most famous and enduring of these leaders was John Langalibalele Dube, born in 1871 at the Inanda station of the American Zulu Mission. His father was an ordained priest, and his mother was a Christian convert. As was the case with many politically active young blacks, he received his primary education at the hands of the mission and his secondary education at the nearby Adams College, also an American missionary institution. As something of a prodigy, Dube was sponsored by the mission to attend Oberlin College in Ohio, where he fell very much under the influence of the black American civil rights leader Booker T. Washington. Dube was impressed particularly with the concept of industrial education and the "learn to walk before you can run" approach to black emancipation and postbellum reconstruction.

**Dube**

Returning to South Africa with this concept at the fore of his mind, Dube established the first, fully indigenous educational institute, the Zulu Christian Industrial School, also known as Ohlange High School. Incidentally, this school, was located close to Gandhi's Phoenix settlement, and although the two organizations promoted a similar agenda and overlapped in much that they did, they did not associate or cooperate.

Solomon Tshekisho Plaatje was another seminal figure of the early black political movement in South Africa. A few years younger than John Dube, Sol Plaatje is often described as the first prominent black academic in South Africa. He was a Tswana, but he relocated to the Cape just before the Boer War, and was, as a consequence, something of a product of liberal Cape tradition. Born in the Orange Free State in 1876, he too was the product of a missionary background, although in his case, German Lutheran missionaries, and his education was also missionary sponsored. He also became proficient as a pianist and violinist, a composer and writer, and fluent in numerous languages. He was perhaps most influential, however, as a journalist, novelist, and political polemicist. His criticism of the South Africa Act of 1909 was entitled "Sekgoma – the Black Dreyfus," a commanding piece of political literature that remained unpublished until relatively recently. An admirer of Marcus Garvey rather than Booker

T Washington, he was part of the intellectual black elite, and, like his other hero, W.E.B. Du Bois, he urged the intellectualism of blacks as an avenue of liberation.

**Plaatje**

   As South African blacks began the establishment of a mass nationalist movement, various articles and instruments of discriminatory legislation began popping up on the Union statute. The strikes of 1913 had much to do with the economics of white and black labor, and the outrage caused among whites by economically conscious mine owners employing skilled black labor at a cheaper rate than skilled white labor. In 1911, the "Mines and Works Act" reserved certain categories of labor and most skilled positions for whites. Also in 1911, the "Native Land Regulation Act" made it law for blacks injured in industrial accidents to receive less compensation than their white colleagues. It was also legislated that they could be held criminally responsible for strikes or any breach of contracts, and it prohibited blacks from military service.

   In 1913, under intense pressure from their rural constituency, the government of Botha and Smuts introduced and piloted through parliament the "Land Act," which began the campaign of limiting black access to land. It prohibited the purchase or lease of land by blacks outside the native reserves. The "native reserves" at that point were not a formal concept but often simply comprised land, such as in Zululand, upon which the tribes were left in possession of some portion of their original land. There, in theory, their traditional lifestyles could be protected and retained.

The Land Act served several purposes, but it was primarily intended to limit and control black access to land, and also, as a corollary, to solve a growing labor problem in industry and mining. It limited the movement of blacks outside of the reserves without a legal "pass," which was only issued upon proof that an individual was employed by a white person. It was understood, and indeed hoped, that limited space and resources in the native reserves would force blacks into the cities on labor contracts, but at the same time, rather ironically, the cities and towns remained strictly designated as white-only areas.

South African "pass" laws were probably the most odious and discriminatory articles of differentiating legislation in an environment of increasingly restrictive laws and conventions related to race. The first use of documentation identifiable as a "pass" was in the early 1800s, and various laws and statutes were enacted during the latter part of the century as diamonds and gold began to introduce a culture of formal labor and triggered the widespread migration and movement of blacks to the centers of mining and industry. Under these statutes, the term "black" often simply meant non-white, and the story is told of Gandhi as a young Indian barrister in Pretoria acquiring a special permit from the state attorney of the Transvaal to allow him to enter Pretoria without specific documentation proving that he was employed by a white person. He was, of course, employed by an Indian and not a European, which was a difficulty. An interesting fact is that the Transvaal Attorney general at that time was a Jewish lawyer trained in London and a member of the same bar association as Gandhi.

Gandhi's predicament fell under the laws and statutes of the Transvaal Republic, which, although draconian, were nonetheless haphazardly applied and seldom enforced. Under British rule, the same laws became subject to British standards of enforcement and administration, and Gandhi noted that life, commerce, and the free movement of non-whites became infinitely more difficult once Milner's Kindergarteners had assumed control of the local bureaucracy.

In 1923, the infamous "Natives (Urban Areas) Act" was debated and passed in the Union legislature, formally designating the urban area of the Union as white. Thereafter, it was required that all black South Africans, regardless of origin, carry pass and identification documents at all times. This began to establish a precedent, and the enforcement of separate urban amenities quickly began to take effect. White-only facilities, from railways to busses to beaches, became a feature of daily life in South Africa.

Much of this was driven not so much by the government as by the right-wing constituency that was steadily gathering pace and gathering influence under the leadership of James Hertzog. In the general election of 1924, Smuts, who had been Prime Minister of South Africa since

September 1919, was defeated by Hertzog's National Party, and with that, the first overtly racist Afrikaner right-wing nationalist party took office.

**Hertzog**

### The Rise of the Right

Botha died in August 1919 of heart failure, and upon his death, his natural heir was Smuts, who was just returning from his triumphant term as a member of the British War Cabinet and his service on the various drafting committees of the Treaty of Versailles. As deputy, Smuts took office upon the death of the incumbent prime minister, and two years later in 1921, he fought a general election. His main opponent was Hertzog, standing as the National Party candidate and representing the right-wing of the Afrikaner nationalist movement. Smuts stood as the South African Party candidate, and his platform was essentially pro-British and imperialist.

Although Smuts triumphed reasonably easily, the National Party returned a respectable result. Smuts campaigned mainly on his status as the great war general and member of various lofty imperial political forums. However, as would continue to be the case throughout his life, Smuts, while deeply admired in the imperial context, was rather reviled at home. He was acknowledged in Britain and the United States as a great international statesman, an architect of European peace, and a founder of the League of Nations, but locally he remained somewhat under a cloud for precisely the same reasons. Although his achievements on the imperial stage certainly elevated the status of South Africa, they seemed to attract criticism at home, and his close engagement with the British certainly undermined crucial support from among his own Afrikaans-speaking community.

Smuts was quite aware of what a National Party victory in South Africa might mean, and while he made concessions to the right in terms of numerous articles of discriminatory legislation, he was not of the school of thought that segregation was the solution to the emerging "native problem." He was an advocate of the "Sacred Trust," the verbiage of which he himself inserted into the Covenant of the League of Nations.[16] The "Sacred Trust," in the context of the British Empire as a whole, was an acknowledgment that Africa existed fundamentally as an African realm, and that it was the trust and responsibility of the governing race to guide the black man toward parity and equal representation with fairness and honesty. On the surface, there might appear to be scant difference between this position and the segregationist position of Hertzog, for both espoused separate developments. However, the two positions differed a great deal in intent. The former was inspired by a belief in the rights and ambitions of the emerging black political movement (albeit acknowledging that the moment was not precisely now), while the latter was constructed on antipathy, racism, and a determination to never allow the black man to rise above the current status.

Facing a second general election, Smuts looked around for a solution, and his eye fell on the northern territory of Southern Rhodesia. The territory was administered by a private chartered company, the British South Africa Company, whose charter was due to expire in 1925, and the question of what system of government would replace it was very much at the center of the public debate in Southern Rhodesia. Three options existed, with the first being an amalgamation of Northern and Southern Rhodesia. The second was a responsible government of its own, and the third was an absorption into the Union of South Africa as a fifth province.

---

[16] It was the 'Sacred Trust' that underwrote the League of Nations Mandate system. Territory's were held in trust until the conditions for independence were in place.

As these options were being considered, Smuts realized that if Southern Rhodesia could be persuaded to cast its lot in with South Africa, he would acquire a bloc of about 35,000 fanatically loyal British imperial voters who would certainly swing the next general election back around to the liberal, pro-imperial position. He made a generous offer of cash and political representation, and there were certainly a great many Southern Rhodesians who were tempted, but South Africa had certain problems that the pro-British Southern Rhodesians worried about as well. For example, South Africa had a large population of poor whites, and it was feared that they may well flood into Southern Rhodesia in search of cheap land. The legacy of the Boer War also concerned the whites of the northern colony.

In the end, it was the violent and bitter labor unrest of the early 1920s that turned the Southern Rhodesian electorate away. Since the end of the Boer War and the Chinese labor crisis, the mining industry in South Africa emerged as a hotbed of race and labor politics. The essence of the strikes of 1913 and 1914 was the tendency of mine owners to make use of cheap, black skilled and unskilled labor in preference to higher paid white labor. After World War I, however, the mining industry faced renewed challenges and acute financial problems. It was an age of high inflation, and the mines were beginning to operate at much deeper levels, thus incurring significantly greater costs. One glaring anomaly in the industries balance sheet was the inflated cost for white labor when much cheaper black labor was readily available.

What followed was a series of strikes and labor actions involving white labor, and a popular slogan was "Workers of the World United, and Fight for a White South Africa." Clearly, there was more to these series of strikes and demonstrations than simply wages and working conditions, and as luck would have it, as a delegation from Southern Rhodesia was visiting South Africa on a fact-finding mission, Smuts was forced to act. The strikers, most of whom were Afrikaans-speaking, formed commando units and gave the impression of an armed revolt. Smuts reacted swiftly and resolutely, declaring martial law and deploying troops, tanks, aircraft, and artillery to crush what did indeed quickly turn into a full-scale rebellion. The mild-mannered leader revealed his menacing side, after which the Southern Rhodesia delegation hurried home determined to petition for a responsible government of its own. The end result was that Smuts was indeed swept out of office in the general election of 1924, and the National Party, with Herzog at its helm, took power in South Africa.

Hertzog went to work immediately, entrenching white predominance, passing numerous articles of discriminatory legislation, and promoting the interests of the white Afrikaans community. He also worked to distance South Africa from the British Empire, claiming greater autonomy and proceeding apace with "differentiating" legislation that, under the rules of empire, ought to have attracted a Crown veto. A Land Bank was formed to benefit those of the agricultural community, marketing controls were established, and state-run corporations were created, most notably in the iron and steel industries.

Perhaps the most impactful legislation enfranchised white women, but not black, and while this might be seen on the surface as an advance in representation, it simply eroded the effectiveness of the Cape's qualified franchise. In fact, this represented the first orchestrated assault against it. English was no longer the exclusive language of administration and justice, and as a result, the civil service was opened up to Afrikaans-speakers, beginning a convention of Afrikaans domination of the civil service.

In perhaps an act of more symbolic than practical use, but nonetheless giving a clear indication of the direction in which things were heading, the Afrikaans language was differentiated from Dutch, which the South Africa Act of 1909 listed as the second language of the dominion. Afrikaans had by then developed rather separately from Dutch and was truly a unique and separate language. This acknowledgment also recognized the uniqueness of Afrikaans culture as an intrinsically and identifiable African culture. By 1925, the Bible had been translated into Afrikaans, followed by an Afrikaans dictionary and, in due course, a substantial body of Afrikaans literature.

While not necessarily an Afrikaans writer, the career of South African feminist, liberal, and author Olive Schreiner is shines a light on the South African liberal movement. Olive Schreiner was the author of the seminal work *The Story of an African Farm*, which is generally regarded as the first literary work of any renown to come out of South Africa. Olive Schreiner was a fiercely liberal activist at the dawn of liberal feminism, and as a member of the Cape Dutch community, she led the extreme liberal fringe, which consisted of her brother William and another Cape liberal feminist, Elizabeth Molteno. Both women were friends and supporters of Gandhi during his period of South African activism, and both campaigned relentlessly for a free and egalitarian society. Olive Schreiner died in 1920 as these events were taking place, but the white, liberal tradition in South Africa was certainly alive and well.

**Schreiner**

In 1926, Hertzog attended his first Imperial Conference as South African prime minister, and there, in the company of his colleagues from Britain, Canada, New Zealand, and Australia, he campaigned for a complete reevaluation of the relationship between Britain and the dominions. This motion was well received among the other dominions, for if nothing else, World War I had redefined the status of the empire in relation to its dependent territories, few of which were in practical terms dependent anymore. Thereafter, the dominions regarded and defined themselves as autonomous communities of the British Empire, sharing a common allegiance to the Crown.

In regard to the other three dominions, this was stating the obvious, and Whitehall did not particularly object, but the situation in South Africa was rather different. The native races of Australia or Canada were never serious contenders for power, and their numbers were so small that the removal of their right of autonomy did not represent any particular conundrum. Africans across the diaspora, however, were more politically alert and present in significant numbers. The

"Sacred Trust" demanded that Britain protect the interests of the black majority with a view to a future of majority rule, but that would be rather difficult to enforce in South Africa. Settler communities all over Africa had been placed on notice that the British regarded Africa as African, but this was enormously complicated in South Africa by the fact that the energized Afrikaner movement also presented itself as African.

In 1931, the Statute of Westminster was passed, giving legal force to a new inter-imperial relationship. By then, all the dominions had begun acting independently in international affairs, placing diplomats in foreign capitals and diminishing the powers and roles of their territorial governor. In 1934, the "Status of the Union Act" was debated and passed by the South African Parliament, underlining and reinforcing the Statute of Westminster. For instance, it provided that acts of the British Parliament would no longer be valid in South Africa unless they were also enacted by the South African Parliament, and that the governor-general should act exclusively on the advice of his South African ministers.

During this time, the Great Depression was acutely felt in South Africa, which was primarily a gold producer and exporter. Hertzog resolutely held the South African pound to the gold standard while Britain and the other dominions devalued their currency. As a result, South African exports, especially wool exports, almost ceased, and by the time the South African pound was devalued in December 1932, the economy had been seriously damaged. This drove Hertzog to the negotiating table with Smuts, from which emerged the United Party, with a breakaway Afrikaans-speaking faction led by Daniel F Malan, calling itself, rather ominously, the Purified National Party.

**Malan**

Hertzog next turned his attention to the Cape qualified franchise, which had been the target of his ire since the National Convention. In 1936, the Native Representation Act was passed, deeply eroding and compromising native representation by removing all black voters from the ordinary voters roll. The legislation also gave black voters only the right to vote for three members to sit in the House of Assembly, the dominant forum at that time, to represent their interests. In all four provinces, blacks could similarly elect white representation, while a Native Advisory Council was established with advice-giving powers.

By now, the race struggle was beginning to coalesce in the cities and towns as desperate blacks, marginalized from state assistance during the Great Depression, flooded into the urban areas in defiance of the pass laws. In 1919, the Industrial and Commercial Workers Union was formed, and in 1921, the Communist Party of South Africa came together. In 1930, both organizations began a campaign of pass burning that attracted a mass participation of blacks and Indians in every urban center of the country. In Durban, one protest was stormed by police and four people were killed.

Clearly, a mood of militancy was spreading in black South Africa, and this had the effect of entrenching white resistance to change, mostly in the right-wing, Afrikaans-speaking community. The English-speaking portion of the white population, although hardly liberal, was somewhat less hardline. Nonetheless, the problem was universal insofar as there were few whites who seriously contemplated offering blacks direct representation or opening administrative jobs to black civil servants. A certain amount of traditional leadership was tolerated in the reserves, but no interest to speak of existed when it came to extending matters further than that.

The Purified National Party was now the voice of the Afrikaner fringe, a movement that attracted an alarmingly wide popular response. A generation of marginalized white Afrikaners who survived the Boer War but lost everything were by the 1930s beginning to establish positions of security, wealth, and influence, and their numbers were swelling faster than the English-speaking white community. Numerous Afrikaner cultural movements emerged, celebrating Afrikaner history and such epic events as the Great Trek and the Battles of Blood River and Vegkop. Nonetheless, in the 1938 general election, the United Party won 111 seats in the National Assembly, while Malan's Purified National Party won just 27.

## World War II and the Triumph of Afrikaner Nationalism

At the end of the decade, an economic recovery was underway, the economy was booming, and for both black and white South Africans, wages climbed, standards of living improved, and the United Party consolidated its grip on the apparatus of government. However, just over the horizon, the first great test of South African autonomy within the British Commonwealth began to manifest. The growing militancy of Nazi Germany presaged war, which in turn reignited the debate of who would and who would not stand with Britain. The participation of Australia, New Zealand, and Canada would never be doubted, but for South Africa, it prompted another agonizing bout of soul-searching.

When Britain declared war on Germany, the United Party, now fundamentally defined by the personalities of Hertzog and Smuts, split along precisely those lines. Smuts, of course, was immediately committed to declaring South Africa for the Allies, while Hertzog was no less adamant that South Africa owed Britain no such commitment. In a passionate debate in the House of Assembly, Hertzog argued for South African neutrality, but when a vote was taken, he was roundly defeated. The governor-general refused his request to dissolve parliament and call a general election, leading to Hertzog's resignation. This paved the way for Smuts to serve a second term as Prime Minister of South Africa and to lead South Africa into the war.

The main theaters of South African involvement in World War II were in East Africa, North Africa, and Italy. Individual South African servicemen signed up with numerous imperial regiments, and South African pilots were very well represented in the Royal Air Force.

The East Africa Campaign of World War II was quite different than the fighting a generation earlier. This time, the threat came from the Italians entrenched in Ethiopia and Somalia. Mussolini nurtured an ambition to extend the Italian overseas empire by driving the British out of East Africa and rolling the Italian army as far south as possible. A combined Allied force, dominated by South Africans, launched a campaign in the summer of 1940 that broke Italian resistance almost immediately, driving them back to Addis Ababa in just a few months. Commanding one of the attacking columns was South African Major General Dan Pienaar.

From there, the focus of the war shifted to North Africa, where South African units were scattered across the various imperial commands. As the war then moved up through the boot of Italy, South African tank crews were present. By the end of the war, some 218,000 South Africans were in uniform, and of these, 13,000 were women, 27,000 were "colored" men, and 42,000 were black. All were volunteers. Black and colored men tended to be distributed among the various white detachments and labor and transport drivers, although a handful did manage to find their way into combat units. All the while, the white backlash proved intense. While the soldiers found themselves on common ground in battle, back home, the likes of Daniel Malan fulminated against the use of "Kaffir" soldiers. Despite this, of the 5,500 South Africans killed during the war, more than a quarter were black.

During the war, Smuts was again brought into the British War Cabinet in an advisory role, this time joining a panel of similar experts and senior imperial statesmen advising British Prime Minister Winston Churchill. He was given the honorary rank of British Field Marshal, and he was again celebrated in the halls of imperial power. Upon his death in 1950, his statue was placed in Parliament Square in London alongside Churchill, Gandhi, and many other major British imperial figures. This, however, simply added to the ongoing discontent in the Afrikaner nationalist community over his apparent collaboration .

During the war, South Africa also offered the Allies the benefit of a strong arms industry, strategic ports, and a good economy. During the German blockade of the Mediterranean in 1941, the route around the Cape of Good Hope was vital for transporting troops and supplying the Allies in North Africa. South African industry provided munitions, food, clothing, and tobacco, while the products of South Africa's Iron and Steel Corporation, or ISCOR, supported the British munitions and arms industry.

Of course, South African gold and platinum were also quite importance. Gold remained the central prop of the South African economy, employing upwards of 320,000 blacks and 43,000 whites. In 1946, the industry produced £102 million in gold bullion. Close behind was the South African coal industry, and while it remained a major base metal and mineral producer, the South African manufacturing base also expanded and grew at a healthy pace. By the end of the war, the South African garment industry employed 70,000 people and produced goods worth £42 million.

All of this tended to further urbanize the population, to the extent that by the end of the war, about 75% of the population lived and worked in an urban area, including at least 24% of blacks. This was a significant figure, because, although a smaller percentage, it meant that urban blacks outnumbered both urban whites and Indians in pure numbers.

Moreover, the character and status of blacks in the cities was changing. In 1911, a census was conducted that put 55% of blacks present in urban areas as contract workers or migrant labor whose homes were elsewhere. By 1946, it was found that less than 21% of blacks in cities were employed by the traditional exploiters of migrant labor, with the remainder in permanent or semi-permanent residence and distributed across a broad-based employment market ranging from domestic to commercial to industrial.

In tandem with these changes, more blacks became literate, with an increasing number getting educations. A major demographic shift was underway that saw blacks abandoning the overcrowded and impoverished reserves and flocking to the cities in unregulated droves. The irony, as many observed at the time, was that successful economic policies were acting against social policies that were aimed at keeping blacks out of the cities and in the reserves. Thus, even as the policies incentivized blacks to come, no provisions were made for them when they arrived. The purchase or rent of property in an urban area was impossible for blacks, so shanty towns began to appear on the outskirts of the main industrial towns and cities, especially the industrial metropolis of Johannesburg.

With this state of affairs, a vibrant African urban culture grew, but it also fostered enormous discontent, violence, and crime. The cost of living began to creep up as young blacks found meager employment in the informal economy, women ran "shebeens" and distilled and brewed illicit alcohol, prostitution was rife, and violent crime was endemic.[17] At the same time, the government's "civilized labor" policy remained in effect, providing sheltered employment for whites, with unskilled white labor earning on average more than twice the wages of unskilled black labor.

If World War I rattled the imperial establishment and weakened it at the knees, it was World War II that finished it off. By the latter half of the 1940s, as India was granted independence, the nationalist political movement across Africa was energized and began to gather momentum. A combination of returning black servicemen (many of whom had served in Burma and had absorbed the airs of Indian independence) and a growing generation of educated and political youth started a powerful African liberation movement. The center of this in South Africa was the seething babel of languages, ethnicities, and backgrounds of the Witwatersrand mining compounds. The rotation of migrant labor from all over the region created a highly mobile market for ideas and ideologies in an environment that was intensely reactionary and political. Strikes became more and more frequent as black labor unions and organizations began to flex their muscles. Despite an Industrial Conciliation Act that forbade black involvement in collective bargaining and declared strikes illegal, blacks still organized, and in 1945, the Council of Non-European Trade Unions boasted a membership of 158,000 spread across some 119 separate unions.

---

[17] A 'shebeen' is a back street bar selling bootleg liquor and illegally brewed beer.

The front-line of the emerging struggle, of course, remained the mine compounds and shanty towns of Johannesburg and the Witwatersrand. Here, the politics of black nationalism flourished and formed. Between 1939 and 1948, the Native Affairs Department received reports of over one hundred gold and coal industry industrial actions. The largest of these was a four-day strike called by the African Mineworker's Union in August 1936. Some 74,000 workers brought the industry in the Witwatersrand to a standstill over the government's refusal to implement reforms recommended by a government commission.

The government's reaction was swift and violent. Strike leaders were arrested, 12 were killed, and 1,200 injured. The government held to the position that while union organization among whites was beneficial, among blacks it encouraged mindless and reactionary behavior, proving that blacks simply lacked the maturity to organize and express grievances in a peaceful and controlled manner. The African Mineworker's Union was effectively emasculated, and the Council of Non-European Trade Union was deeply compromised.

Smuts, as the leader of this repressive movement, did so very much against his better judgment, and often the highly fluid nature of the situation resulted in reactionary and haphazard policy. Smuts has often been lumped together with the white nationalists as being responsible for this policy, but by then he was no longer the architect of events. The principles of segregation continued to be espoused in the various articles of legislation – the Representation of Natives Act of 1936, the Native Trust and Land Act of 1936, and the Native Laws Amendment Act of 1937 – but in most respects, Smuts was pressing forward in the dark. He was hardly a liberal, but he was certainly not a visceral racist. Uncertain what the future held, he was clueless as to how to contain the situation without revealing quite how out of step with the times he was.

As all of this was taking place, Smuts was summoned one last time to contribute to the establishment of the United Nations as the successor to the League of Nations. He was instrumental in the wording of the United Nations Declaration of Human Rights, which must have been extremely difficult bearing in mind the regular and unapologetic flaunting by his own government of these very principles. By then, the forum was dominated by the likes of India and other independent states, and he suffered open criticism for South Africa's repressive race policies. Smuts was forced to acknowledge the hypocrisy of the situation, and it was a relief to him not to be asked to contribute in the same way again.

Behind the scenes, a growing corps of white academics and professionals urged the government to nip the revolution in the bud by increasing black wages, recognizing black trade unions, and abolishing the hated pass laws. The business sector also tended to echo these sentiments, urging the creation of a stable labor market. White members of parliament elected to express black concerns argued consistently for reforms, and some mainstream members of parliament began to argue in cautious terms for the removal of any color clauses from the constitution.

International disapprobation was also gathering stream. The Atlantic Charter, signed by President Roosevelt and Churchill in 1941, marked the entry of the United States into World War II, but with certain conditions. The independence and sovereignty of all peoples was a basic criterion, which signaled the end of the British Empire and the European imperial period as a whole. The establishment of the United Nations and the independence of India marked an age of emancipation, and as the liberation struggle gathered momentum across Africa, South Africa became a more prominent target for the growing liberation and anti-imperialist movement.

In South Africa, this unleashed a wave of tepid and ineffectual commissions of inquiry into everything from urban living conditions to the long-term effect of migrant labor, and through the process, the full extent of social rot was exposed. Smuts was forced to concede that segregation as a workable social policy was moot, but he was aging and bereft of answers, and his government did not have much to offer as a solution. A report published in 1948 by Justice Henry Allan Fagan concluded that the trend toward black urbanization was irreversible, adding that the system of pass laws was unworkable. Instead, a labor bureau would be more useful in directing labor to where it was most needed.

Smuts' helplessness, and the wave of practical and useful advice that could not be utilized, all pointed to the fact that race policy in South Africa was no longer driven by practicality, if it ever had been. It was now due solely to dogma and ideology, in which case a working solution was not particularly possible. White wages remained inflated, artificial barriers of separation supported white privilege, and almost 20 times more was spent per capita on white education than black.

Despite all the barriers, black political organizations were reaching a standard of maturity and effectiveness that represented a direct and unavoidable challenge to white hegemony. In 1943, at the annual conference of the African National Congress, a challenge was issued to the government in the form of a statement entitled African Claims in South Africa. Citing the Atlantic Charter, it traced out a bill of rights calling for an end to discrimination, redistribution of land, black participation in collective bargaining, and universal adult suffrage.

Nothing struck quite so directly to the core of white anxiety than universal adult suffrage, and the more these calls were made, the more determined the white establishment became in ensuring that it never happen. In 1944, the ANC Youth League was founded by Walter Sisulu and Oliver Tambo, two seminal figures in the movement. The founding of the Youth League introduced a new and radical generation of black politicians, and into their midst arrived a young attorney by the name of Nelson Mandela.

For its part, the Afrikaner movement was also groping toward what it sensed as a moment of national realization. The agricultural sector of the economy remained largely in Afrikaans hands, and Afrikaans-speakers were emerging in the English-speaking milieu of the cities, academia, professions, business, and industry. Numerous Afrikaans cultural and political organizations emerged. The *Broederbond*, the *Federasie van Afrikaanse Kultuurverenigings* (Federation of Afrikaner Cultural Associations), the Afrikaner churches, and the *Reddingsdaadbond* (Rescue Association) were just a few of these, and the National Party was the political party under which it all resided. On the far right, fringe organizations such as the *Ossewa Brandwag* (Oxwagon Sentinel) openly supported Nazi Germany during World War II and espoused a more radical and potentially oppressive race policy.

The *Ossewa Brandwag* did not speak for the majority, but it nonetheless signaled the rise of the Afrikaner right and an era of bold and defiant Afrikaner attitudes as the world was mostly rallying against such outdated social and political ideologies. Daniel Malan, the far-right leader of the Purified National Party, led the Afrikaner movement, and as the 1948 general election loomed, he campaigned vigorously with growing confidence. While other sectors of the political establishment fractured and subsided into irrelevance, the National Party was able to unite Afrikaans-speakers from across the spectrum. A powerful sense of nationalism emerged against a backdrop of republicanism, and the rise of a people brutally defeated half a century earlier in a war with the British. Race paranoia was also a powerful force, in particular among the working classes who sensed daily a threat to their protected status by a rising black working class and intelligentsia. The word "apartheid," or "apartness," became a word more frequently coined in the race debate, and while it was not yet a policy, it was surely a sign of the times.

By contrast, the United Party offered up a vague and ill-formed series of policies, espoused by Smuts who, at 78, was increasingly old and out of touch. Besides that, it forced him onto the back foot by having to deal with and rationalize the growth of urban migration, and in a situation where no practical or accepted policy could hope to satisfy a majority of the electorate, the advantage lay with the opposition. A general election was held on May 26, 1948, and the National Party, led by Daniel Malan, emerged with 70 seats (mainly rural) to the United Party's 65 (mainly urban). Smuts conceded defeated and slipped gratefully into retirement, dying two years later as South Africa separated itself from the British Empire and the policies of apartheid began to shape the direction of life and government.

On June 1, 1948, Daniel Malan arrived in Pretoria by train to take office, and there he was met by a huge crowd of cheering whites. He told the audience, "In the past, we felt like strangers in our own country, but today, South Africa belongs to us once more. For the first time since Union, South Africa is our own. May God grant that it always remain our own."

Back in Johannesburg, the leadership of the ANC, including the young attorney Nelson Mandela, listened to these celebratory prognostications in a grim mood. As strangers in their own country, they all understood that the South African liberation struggle would not be won overnight.

## Implementing Apartheid

The iconic 1948 General Election in South Africa that projected Daniel Malan and the right-wing Afrikaner National Party to power also marked a parting of the ways between the Union of South Africa and Britain. Notwithstanding its status as a British overseas dominion, Whitehall had not been in a position to exert meaningful influence on the political process in South Africa for years. Indeed, residual British political influence in any of the overseas dominions amounted to very little, and Canada, Australia, and New Zealand all entered the postwar period with almost absolute autonomy. South Africa stood apart from the other dominions, less as an expression of independence or self-sufficiency than simple defiance. British policy in Africa was to prepare the ground for a domestic African takeover, but that was never going to fly in South Africa. South African independence meant independence under white rule, not black, and every international forum watched in dismay as South Africa entrenched white minority rule and settled in for the long haul.

The final break came in 1961, after a decade of rancorous relations, when South Africa declared itself a republic, replacing the old imperial with standard diplomatic relations with Britain. South Africa's membership in the Commonwealth was withdrawn after a majority of members objected, at which point South Africa effectively separated from the British Empire and every residual imperial association that continued to exist.

At this stage, the Republic of South Africa was more than the sum of its parts. South Africa was emerging as a regional economic and military superpower, registering almost meteoric economic growth, and it enjoyed burgeoning wealth and a rate of development that outpaced the rest of sub-Saharan Africa to a fantastic degree. One particular American diplomat was heard to remark that by world standards, the South African communications infrastructure was excellent, but by African standards it was miraculous. While this was certainly true, and while it was aided by an incorruptible administrative bureaucracy, it was nonetheless built on a hopelessly skewed social and fiscal economy.

In the aftermath of its 1948 electoral victory, the National Party quickly moved to consolidate power. Parliamentary seats were added to represent South West Africa, on the one hand, both formalizing South African control of the territory and bolstering the right wing, which was well represented in the UN-mandated territory. It then finished the assault against the Cape-qualified franchise begun by James Hertzog. All coloreds were removed from the common voters roll, relegating their voice to the same level as blacks by empowering them only to elect white parliamentary representatives to represent their interests. Coloreds represented a large voting body who were typically loyal to the United Party, but they were now excluded from the franchise.

The United Party, after the 1948 defeat and the death of Smuts in 1950, began to wither, while the National Party grew steadily in strength and influence.[18] For the next 20 years, the "Nats" swept successive general elections, building upon a solid economic performance and rising standards of living to eventually win the loyalty of even English-speaking whites. This was only, in part, a reaction to the steady economic growth, because it was also thanks to the emergence and integration of the Afrikaans elite and the marshaling of a common white response to African liberation movements elsewhere on the continent. By 1960, the National Party enjoyed a virtual monopoly on power, but the Belgian Congo was independent, and the spectacle of a generally ordered and well-run colony descending into unrestrained bloodletting and anarchy within months convinced white South Africans across the board that the same must never happen south of the Limpopo. The Nats appeared to have a firm grip on the race issue in South Africa, and most whites were either supportive of or prepared to overlook the rise of apartheid as the price of security in a turbulent age.

As this all indicates, the National Party was in many respects also a cultural movement, promoting first and foremost the interests of the Afrikaner nation. The institutions of state and government were steadily packed with Afrikaans speakers, until the cabinet, the civil service, the judiciary, the police, army, and all state corporations were dominated by Afrikaans speakers. This would have important ramifications later when apartheid began to gather notoriety and general disapprobation, by which time the system was so thoroughly in Afrikaner hands that even international and local condemnation could not force change. Of course, the steady support of the Afrikaner cultural movement also led to the rise to power and wealth of a great many Afrikaans speakers, who by the 1960s had reached a state of parity in regard to the economic and social influence of English speakers. There were many prominent Afrikaans academics, authors, artists, and captains of industry, and the differences of class that in the past had separated the languages no longer existed to the same degree.

In 1961, the single greatest Afrikaner cultural goal was achieved when, after a narrow referendum victory, the government declared South Africa a republic, 60 years after the signing of the Treaty of Vereeniging. After a backlash from almost every member, South Africa withdrew from the British Commonwealth with little apparent regret. The cries of anguish from the civilized world were regarded as a fair price to pay for the restoration of the scared Afrikaner republic.

Economically, South Africa defied the already established African model by registering steady growth and diversification. It has often been remarked that the South African economy was a law unto itself, growing robustly through the 1950s, 1960s, and 1970s despite a backward-looking and repressive government. Much of this had to do with South African gold, which continued to form the central pillar of the economy. South Africa, as a consequence, wielded a comparatively unassailable military strength in Africa, not to mention an economic ballast that would not easily be upset.

---

[18] The United Part was dissolved in 1977

Whites were the principal beneficiaries of all of this, and the National Party applied no less diligence to its flagship program of assuring white supremacy in the country. Most of the early work to achieve this amounted to bolstering and supporting existing segregationist legislation and tightening up the enforcement of those laws. This began the policy that would later be formally identified as "apartheid."

The word apartheid, meaning simply separation or segregation, entered the South African political dictionary in 1929 with the publication of a Dutch Reform Church manifesto suggesting a system of racial separation and using the term apartheid. The date of origin of segregation in South Africa has tended to be identified as 1913 with the publication of the "Native Lands Act," which began the regulation of black land ownership and the statutory separation of the races. In 1936, the "Native Trust and Land Act" was published, enlarging the native reserves from just over 7% of the total landmass of the country to a little over 13%. Appropriating the Persian suffix term "-stan," meaning land, and "Bantu," the aggregate term "Bantustan" was coined to refer to regions of the country set aside as nominally independent black homelands.

The true architect of apartheid, if there was a particular culprit, was Prime Minister Hendrik Frensch Verwoerd. Verwoerd led South Africa from 1958-1966, prior to which he managed the Department of Native Affairs, and it was he who indelibly imprinted the doctrine of apartheid on the South African legal statute. Verwoerd arrived in South Africa in 1903 as the two-year-old son of pro-Boer Dutch parents and grew up mainly in Cape Town, developing a passionate identification with the emerging Afrikaner movement. After earning a doctorate in phycology from Stellenbosch University, he remained on the academic staff as a professor of applied psychology. All the while, he was active in politics, promoting a white, Afrikaans agenda and opposing the immigration of Jewish refugees into South Africa during the Nazi occupation of Europe. He entered politics as an appointed senator under Daniel Malan and served as Prime Minister until his assassination in 1966.

**Verwoerd**

During those crucial eight years, Verwoerd oversaw the transformation of South Africa into the most racially polarized nation on earth. By the time he was leading the country, most of the legal framework to support apartheid was already in place, and all that was required was vigorous enforcement to ensure complete separation of the races. Verwoerd made numerous speeches and public declarations in support of the policy of apartheid, and as a doctor of phycology, his view of the race landscape was informed by his academic experience. He said the following in a speech in December 1950: "My point is this that, if mixed development is to be the policy of the future of South Africa, it will lead to the most terrific clash of interests imaginable. The endeavors and desires of the Bantu and the endeavors and objectives of all Europeans will be antagonistic. Such a clash can only bring unhappiness and misery to both. Both Bantu and European must, therefore, consider in good time how this misery can be averted from themselves and from their descendants. They must find a plan to provide the two population groups with opportunities for the full development of their respective powers and ambitions without coming into conflict. The only possible way out is the second alternative, namely, that both adopt a development divorced from each other. That is all that the word 'apartheid' means."

At the heart of apartheid lay four distinct concepts. These were that South Africa comprised four racial groups – black, colored, Indian, and white – and that the interests of whites, as the "civilized" race, must prevail over all others. In addition, whites were to hold a monopoly in state and government, and the white race ultimately formed a single nation. Obviously, a white monopoly of political power was the central pillar of the apartheid ideology, and there was no longer any mention of the British Empire's "Sacred Trust," which was supposed to steward the nation and transition it into majority black leadership. Instead, apartheid ensured that the black man must henceforth accept his second-class status as a perpetual state of affairs.

In 1950, while Verwoerd was serving as Minister of Native Affairs, the "Population Registration Act" was passed, providing the legal machinery to allocate each individual a racial category. The methods applied to determine that category could be both arbitrary and Orwellian. One notorious method was to place a pencil in a person's hair, which, if it fell out, would determine that individual as white, but if it remained, would classify the individual as black or colored. The application of this law often split families along lines of classification, and as desperate as marginal whites were not to slide down the scale to a classification of "colored," coloreds strove to ascend the same scale to improve their prospects by a classification of "white."

Similar acts included the "Immorality Act" and the "Prohibition of Mixed Marriages Act" of 1949, which all tended to regulate and sometimes complicate the lives of people living at the point of overlap among the different races. Marriage and sexual relationships between the races, always frowned upon, were henceforth illegal. In 1953, the "Reservation of Separate Amenities Act" was passed, with obvious implications for segregation in the urban areas.

In 1951, the Natives Representation Council, the only officially recognized, nationwide, black administrative institution, was banned. The reserves were then grouped into ten identifiable territories, each designated a "homeland" earmarked for a separate black "nation" governed by traditional leadership under white tutelage. The legal framework to enforce this separation was cleared in 1971 with the passage of the "Bantu Homelands Constitution Act," which empowered the government to grant de facto independence to any homeland, or Bantustan. The Transkei, for example, was declared "self-governing" in 1963 and "independent" in 1976. Bophuthatswana followed in 1977, Venda arrived in 1979, and Ciskei came in 1981. Zululand (or KwaZulu) under the leadership of Chief Mangosuthu Buthelezi, refused to accept independence, and instead, a powerful political front (Inkatha) was established. This formed the basis of the Zulu representative party, the Inkatha Freedom Party.

Citizens of the homelands, thereafter, were stripped of the rights of South African citizenship, although under the existing pass laws, they were allowed free access to the South African labor market, albeit without right of permanent abode. The homelands were often not contiguous, but fragmented, and despite the South African economy continuing to grow, the Bantustans remained economic backwaters and labor pools for South African mining and industry. In regard to this policy, the South African government was quite candid. In a general circular, the Department of Bantu Administration and Development stated, "It is accepted Government policy that the Bantu are only temporarily resident in the European areas of the Republic for as long as they offer their labour there. As soon as they become, for one reason or another, no longer fit for work or superfluous in the labour market, they are expected to return to their country of origin or the territory of the national unit where they fit ethnically if they were not born and bred in their homeland."[19]

**A map of South African Bantustans**

Meanwhile, pass laws were rigorously enforced, and throughout the apartheid era, they remained the most despised aspect of the system for ordinary blacks. No black person could visit a city or urban area for more than 72 hours without the requisite documents, and officials and police were authorized to arrest anyone found doing so. In the 1960s, an annual average of 100,000 people were arrested and processed in this manner, with the number peaking in the mid-1970s to about 380,000. Segregated townships were established on the outer precincts of the cities, while informal and squatter settlements proliferated and were periodically broken up and dispersed. The "Group Areas Act" of 1950, and its many amendments, formally divided the urban areas of South Africa into racial zones where only members of that race might reside. The zoning of white areas obviously held precedent, and the forced removal of incumbent populations to make way for white urban development became a feature of the late 1950s and

[19] Quoted: Thompson, Leonard. *A History of South Africa.* (Yale University Press, New York, 2000) p193

1960s.

Perhaps the most memorable example was "District Six," or the Sixth Municipal District of Cape Town. District Six was a colored neighborhood of Cape Town that could trace its history to the abolition and freeing of slaves of mixed ethnic heritage. In the 1970s, the area was designated white and subsequently leveled, with its population forcibly relocated to designated colored areas of the city. District Six became thereafter something of a cause célèbre and a symbol of the insensitive and high-handed attitude of the government at that time.

Naturally, education was also segregated and controlled. In a rare instance of white segregation, white education was separated along language lines, with Afrikaans schools dealing with Afrikaans speaking students and English schools dealing with English speakers. It was compulsory for a child to attend a school teaching in the language spoken in that child's home. Black education was separated as a matter of policy from the Christian missions, which had long held a monopoly on providing education to blacks. Christian missions were regarded as ideologically suspect, and it was sensed that Christian schools and institutions, with their history of politicization, could not be trusted to maintain a neutral educational doctrine. Under the "Bantu Education Act" of 1953, the government assumed complete control of black education, making it almost impossible for non-government black schools to exist and extending this control to colored and Indian children in the 1960s and 1970s. According to Verwoerd, "Native education should be controlled in such a way that it should be in accord with the policy of the state. If the native in South Africa today in any kind of school in existence is being taught to expect that he will live his adult life under a policy of equal rights, he is making a big mistake. There is no place for him in the European community above the level of certain forms of labour."[20]

In 1959, ignoring significant student and faculty opposition, South Africa's Parliament passed the "Extension of University Education Act," which prohibited the enrollment of black students into mainstream universities without special permission from the relevant cabinet minister. The Native College at Fort Hare was taken over by the government, its staff was replaced, and its role was reestablished as a Xhosa university. Ultimately, Fort Hare would emerge as the gathering place of aspiring black nationalist leaders, educating, among others, Nelson Mandela, Oliver Tambo, Chief Buthelezi, and Robert Mugabe.

Thus, the rise and entrenchment of apartheid in South Africa was backed up by a ruthlessly efficient law and order establishment. This also required a ubiquitous and highly efficient police intelligence network. The National Party government inherited an apparatus of coercion already well established, and along with multiple discriminatory laws came a no less comprehensive raft of punitive laws. The "Suppression of Communism Act," for example, was passed in 1950, offering a broad definition of communism and wide powers to contain it. This was followed by numerous similar laws, including the "Riotous Assemblies Act" of 1956, the "Unlawful

Organizations Act" of 1960, the "Sabotage Act" of 1962, the "General Law Amendment Act" of 1966, the "Terrorism Act" of 1967, and the "Internal Security Act" 1976. This body of legislation delivered vast powers to the police and law and order agencies to arrest without trial. The authorities could also hold detainees indefinitely in solitary confinement, with no obligation to reveal their identities or grant them access to anyone except police and government officials. Any organization could be banned, meetings of any sort could be prohibited, and organizations could be prevented from receiving overseas funding.

### The Birth of the Anti-Apartheid Movement

The international anti-apartheid movement reached its zenith in the late 1980s as the countdown to the end of white domination of South Africa began, but the movement its roots in the early liberalism of the Cape and the advocacy of early liberals such as Olive Schreiner and her brother William. Furthermore, South African churches, with the notable exception of the Dutch Reform Church, the main spiritual platform of the Afrikaner movement, formed a united front against the creeping effects of South African race policy. Soon after the 1948 election, an ecumenical statement was issued condemning apartheid, and in the years that followed, the clergy was often on the at the forefront of the anti-apartheid movement. In 1968, the South African Council of Churches declared apartheid inconsistent with the principles of Christianity.

Initially, the Dutch Reform Church remain steadfastly loyal to the principles of apartheid, but in 1962, a prominent member of the church and a central figure in the "Broederbond," Afrikaner Christiaan Beyers Naudé, broke ranks by founding the Christian Institute. This organization allied white and black Christians, introducing for the first time a multiracial, Christian and academic opposition to official race policies. Naudé and the institute he founded were banned in 1977, but by then opposition to apartheid had begun to find a following within the Dutch Reformed Church, which struck very much at the heart of the Afrikaner nationalist movement.

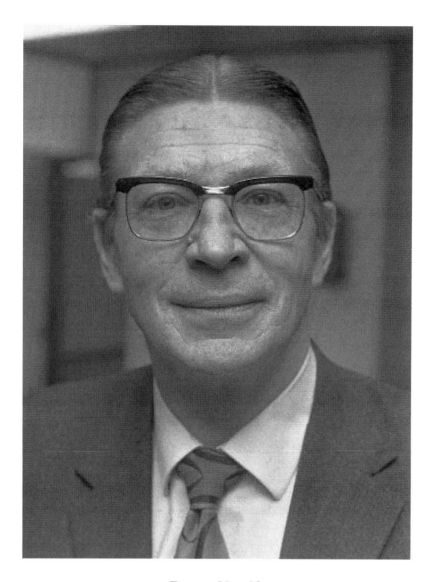

**Beyers Naudé**

The various English-speaking universities, most notably the University of Cape Town and the Witwatersrand University, formed early focal points for the active anti-apartheid movement. The National Union of South African Students was founded in 1924, establishing after 1948 a posture of antagonism toward the government. In 1959, the organization staged a series of rancorous demonstrations against the closure of the established universities to black enrollment. In 1966, US Senator Robert Kennedy visited South Africa as a guest of the organization, bitterly denouncing apartheid during the course of several well-attended speaking engagements.

A more grassroots, domestic white response was founded in 1955 with the "Black Sash," a predominantly white and middle-class women's association. The Black Sash was initially formed to protest the removal of coloreds from the Cape voters roll, but it soon broadened its agenda into a suffragette-style protest movement against government race policies in general. The Black Sash method of protest was to stand with heads bowed, wearing a black sash in symbolic mourning for the death of equality and the constitution, publicly shaming cabinet members and National Party politicians. The movement gained significant following among ordinary white, middle-class women, to the extent that it was formally banned in 1976. It continued to exist, however, as an advisory body, offering legal assistance to blacks caught up in apartheid enforcement and navigating an unequal and unfriendly justice system. Numerous individuals such as authors Alan Paton, Nadine Gordimer, and Athol Fugard voiced their opposition, though at this point big business and industry were too invested in the economic advantages of apartheid to side too openly with the opposition. White labor unions were perhaps the most active supporters of apartheid, simply for the protection the system offered to white labor.

Organized black resistance to apartheid tended to be slower to manifest, simply because life for the average black person under the extremes of apartheid was a consuming struggle to survive. Mass black political organization was yet to find it its feet in a society where every institution of state and government was configured to frustrate it. The most that an individual could do was to adapt to and circumvent the law when possible. In the face of apartheid, a growing black middle class, climbing through the formal economy as nurses, teachers, priests, and skilled workers, were yet to be persuaded that anything was to be gained by protest and resistance. At the same time, the black nationalist movement in South Africa was constrained and frustrated by tribalism, regionalism, and class. In fact, before the National Party takeover in the 1940s, black politics tended to remain the preserve of the educated elite.

The commencement of the wider African liberation movement had the effect of stirring the movement in South Africa. Many of the early African nationalists active to the north of South Africa were men educated in South Africa, often at Fort Hare University, and they were known to the elite of the South African black political movement. As Africa began to stir, so black South Africa awoke. In the early 1950s, at a time when the legal foundations of apartheid were under construction, a new political generation began to come of age. The 1949 annual conference of the ANC, for example, elected three new members - Nelson Mandela, Walter Sisulu, and Oliver Tambo - to the national executive of the ANC Youth League. All three men were products of the mission school system, all were from the Transkei. Mandela, after his expulsion from Fort Hare University, qualified as a lawyer in 1949 after completing a correspondence course at the University of South Africa.[21] Although not among the senior members, Nelson Mandela was nonetheless the dominant member of this group. He was a minor member of the Thembu ruling family in the Transkei and had a commanding personality. He was powerfully built, intelligent, charismatic, and passionately committed to the cause of African liberation.

---

[21] Mandela was expelled from Fort Hare for his political activity and protests.

**Tambo**

The 1952 ANC conference elected Albert Luthuli to the leadership of the ANC, which was a seminal appointment because Luthuli was not of the new generation of educated elites. A modestly educated Zulu traditional leader, he was both forceful and charismatic, and he successfully bridged the divide between the older generation of moderate and somewhat collaborative nationalists and the younger and more radical cadre epitomized by Mandela.

The first major action in this new phase of the struggle was a campaign of passive resistance mounted in partnership with the South African Indian Congress, which had also shed its conservative leadership and emerged in a more radical mood. The campaign began in 1952 and continued for a year before it was called off in the face of a heavy government response, which included the rushing through of severe criminal penalties for the crime of civil disobedience. Rioting in Cape Town, Port Elizabeth, East London, and Johannesburg resulted in the arrest of at least 8,000 activists.

On June 26, 1952, on open ground outside Johannesburg, 3,000 ANC delegates, including 320 Indians and 230 coloreds, met. This gathering formed the basis of the South African Congress Alliance, consisting of the African National Congress, the South African Indian Congress, the

South African Congress of Democrats, and the Colored People's Congress. Before the meeting was broken up by the policy, the "Freedom Charter" was unveiled and adopted. This was an important moment, for the Freedom Charter defined the core principals of the movement and the essential policy statement of the ANC. Its opening demand was, "The People Shall Govern!" It was followed by a further nine similar demands defining the essential freedoms required by a non-subject people. The preamble read, "South Africa belongs to all who live in it, black and white, and that no government can justly claim authority unless it is based on the will of the people."

The government, of course, responded aggressively, bringing to bear the full weight of the law against anyone they could. After thousands were detained without trial, hundreds were tried on spurious charges in lengthy trials intended to both preoccupy the ANC leadership and exhaust its resources. In this way, the government made absolutely clear its intention to not yield one inch, which had the effect of seeding enormous frustration and division within the leadership of the ANC.

Elsewhere in Africa, civil disobedience and violent protests were bringing the British authorities to their knees, and independence seemed to be pending everywhere. Southern Rhodesia was drifting toward war, but for the forces of liberation, it had the potential to be a viable war. To take South Africa to war, however, was a very different prospect. The land borders of South Africa were comparatively short, making the nation easily defensible. Add to that the sheer weight of the South African conventional military machine, and the state was in almost every respect invincible. Internal resistance was the job of the domestic intelligence services to root out, and they were ruthlessly efficient at doing so.

The party was therefore divided along the line of moderates and radicals. The former, led by Albert Luthuli and Nelson Mandela, pressed for dialogue and political pressure, while the hardliners, who were in the majority, increasingly pushed for the formation of an armed wing. Dialogue required a common cause with white liberals, a practice that the radical wing of the ANC believed had damaged the integrity of the struggle. While the doves sought to blur the pure race complexion of the struggle, the hawks sought to clearly and unequivocally identify the enemy as the white man.

This resulted in a split in the ANC and the founding in 1959 of the "Pan-Africanist Congress" (PAC) which would always tend to understudy the ANC but which would still emerge as a powerful and uncompromising voice of the liberation struggle. On March 21, 1960, the PAC staged a national demonstration against the pass laws. The call was widely heeded, and the focal points for popular anger quickly became police stations, where thousands of people presented themselves without pass documents. At a small police sub-station in Sharpeville, part of the Johannesburg conurbation, police opened fire, killing 67 people in arguably the most iconic incident of the opening phase of the "Liberation Struggle." From that moment on, a steadily more forceful and demonstrative popular pushback began to be felt. In the aftermath of Sharpeville, numerous minor, spontaneous popular protests exploded into major demonstrations. The police and security establishment responded with equal resolution, declaring a state of emergency and calling in military reserves.

All of this tended to sharpen the ANC, which, as the senior and larger organization, had always tended to espouse a commitment to passive resistance. Gandhi, upon leaving South Africa for India, had remarked that Africans had no use for passive resistance, vegetarianism, and religion as weapons of war, fully believing the African struggle would be a violent one. The young members of the ANC, Mandela among them, were forced to the same conclusion, and they came to believe that nonviolent methods were a waste of time. As Mandela himself put it during his 1964 trial, "We of the ANC had always stood for a non-racial democracy, and we shrank from any policy which might drive the races further apart than they already were. But the hard facts were that fifty years of non-violence had brought the African people nothing but more and more repressive legislation, and fewer and fewer rights. It would be unrealistic and wrong for African leaders to continue preaching non-violence at a time when the Government met our peaceful demands with force."

In 1961, "Umkhonto we Sizwe" ("Spear of the Nation") was founded as the armed wing of the ANC, and "Poqo" (the "Azanian People's Liberation Army") became the fighting arm of the PAC. Another multiracial militant organization was the "African Resistance Movement," founded in 1960. Collectively, these organizations were responsible for some 200 acts of sabotage, mainly in the form of bombing rural post offices, police stations, and power utilities.

There was an unmistakable flavor of desperate optimism about this phase of the struggle, and ultimately, the state security establishment penetrated and effectively shut down these organizations with ease. On August 5, 1962, the police and state security agents raided an isolated farmhouse near the Natal city of Howick and netted a bonanza. Nelson Mandela was picked up, along with a fellow activist, the white theater director Cecil Williams. A few months later, in December 1963, the iconic Rivonia trial began, and along with several other ANC members, Nelson Mandela was charged with four counts of sabotage and conspiracy to violently overthrow the government.[22]

Mandela made no secret of his involvement in acts of sabotage, thus ensuring a conviction, but with the spirit of a true revolutionary, he turned his trial into a political platform. His speech from the dock has since entered the archive of seminal South African political utterances: "I admit immediately that I was one of the persons who helped to form Umkhonto we Sizwe, and that I played a prominent role in its affairs until I was arrested in August 1962."

It was widely assumed that Mandela would be handed down a death sentence, and he was

---

[22] Mandela's first trial began in October 1963, but it was thrown out for insufficient evidence.

certainly prepared for that, saying, "During my lifetime I have dedicated my life to this struggle of the African people. I have fought against white domination, and I have fought against black domination. I have cherished the ideal of a democratic and free society in which all persons will live together in harmony and with equal opportunities. It is an ideal for which I hope to live for and to see realized. But, my Lord, if it needs be, it is an ideal for which I am prepared to die."

Ultimately, however, the death sentence was commuted to life, and Mandela was briefly held on remand in Johannesburg before his incarceration in the notorious political detention facility of Robbin Island. He would serve 27 years in various South African prisons.

**The inside of Mandela's prison cell**

**The Border War**

When the 1948 general election altered the political direction of South Africa, the United Nations began to express alarm at the tightening grip of South Africa on the UN-mandated territory of South West Africa. At the moment that provincial representation was awarded to South West Africa, it became clear that there was no political will whatsoever in Pretoria to contemplate South West African independence, and while the only pressure for South Africa to do so was political, there was no particular hope of compliance. The 1960s, however, introduced a more militant and aggressive phase of the African struggle, and as arms began to enter the picture, liberation organizations prepared their armed wings and wars began.

Two of the most bitter and long-lived civil wars of that era were in Angola and Mozambique. In both cases, civil war began with a war of independence against the Portuguese, and the Mozambique war of independence was relatively straightforward. A single unity organization, the Frente de Libertação de Moçambique (FRELIMO) challenged the Portuguese government along a single line. In Angola, however, several liberation movements vied for supremacy, including the communist-aligned MPLA, or the People's Movement for the Liberation of Angola, and the right-leaning FNLA, or the National Liberation Front of Angola.[23] The MPLA was supported by Cuba and the Soviet Union, and the FNLA by Zaire and the United States.

The war in Angola, therefore, was an imbroglio that the Portuguese could not ultimately hope to win, but which they nonetheless fought with determination. They were, arguably, the only colonial power in Africa determined to retain control of their overseas provinces. The style of warfare was Maoist, with a combination of terror and propaganda ensuring the loyalty of the surrounding population and forcing Portuguese soldiers to fight on the back foot.

It was under the cover of the civil war in Angola that South West African liberation forces began to infiltrate the northern border areas of future Namibia. The Namibian liberation movement was the South West Africa People's Organization' (SWAPO), which was founded in 1960, and as the Portuguese gradually lost ground, SWAPO insurgents were able to proliferate throughout southern Angola, conducting a low-level counter-insurgency war with the South African Defense Force.

For so long as Portugal remained in substantive control of both Angola and Mozambique and Rhodesia survived, the "Swart Gevaar" ("Black Danger") did not represent a direct threat to South Africa. The South African security response in northern South West Africa remained throughout the 1960s and into the 1970s as a police action, with the SADF and the South African Air Force maintaining a permanent support presence. The situation was radically altered, however, in the spring of 1974, when a left-leaning Portuguese military council overthrew the fascist dictatorship of Marcello Caetano and plunged the Portuguese security policy in southern Africa into confusion. The motivation behind the coup was primarily the bleeding and pointless wars in Angola and Mozambique, and implicit in this was a rapid abandonment of Mozambique and Angola.

In the case of the former, FRELIMO assumed power by preordainment, but in Angola, as the era of Portuguese colonial domination faded away, the various liberation movements fell upon one another, battling for the ultimate prize of power. The situation was now infinitely more complicated. In Mozambique, South Africa applied a policy of destabilization, funding and supporting a pseudo-liberation movement that plunged Mozambique into what would prove to be a 20 year civil war that would ultimately cost tens of thousands of lives and reduce Mozambique to economic ruin.

---

[23] *The third was the National Union for the Total Independence of Angola, or UNITA, founded in 1964.*

In Angola, however, the South African response was more direct and aggressive. The Portuguese departed Angola the moment that it was feasible to do so, handing over power to whoever was present to receive it, and that happened to be the MPLA. The FNLA tended to lose relevance thereafter, but they benefited from an immediate windfall of funding and arms supply from South Africa and the United States. The MPLA, on the other hand, allied to the communist bloc, attracted the immediate interest of the Soviet Union and Cuba. As Soviet arms shipments flooded into Angola, and as Cuban "advisors" began to arrive, the South Africans caught a bout of the jitters, sensing the possibility of a direct conventional threat to South West Africa.

At about the same time, US Secretary of State Henry Kissinger arrived in the region, seeking to bolster the US position in the face of aggressive Soviet and Cuban involvement in Angola.[24] Reluctant in the aftermath of Vietnam to insert American troops directly into Angola, the American government simply poured money in to support the various anti-MPLA factions, but a deal was also struck with South Africa. It was a risky move attempting a war by proxy using a force as discredited as the South African Defense Force, but nonetheless, it was a risk Kissinger was prepared to take. Thus, with covert CIA support, South Africa launched a major invasion of Angola codenamed Operation *Savannah*. At midnight on October 15, 1975, Task Force Zulu, a strong South African battlegroup, crossed from South West Africa into Angola, and within three days, it had advanced to within artillery range of Luanda.

Cuban reinforcements were rushed into Angola and the forces aided by the United States retreated, sensing the grave political risks and leaving the SADF over 1,000 miles in enemy territory. The South African forces were now essentially besieging a city with no objective. Ultimately, the SADF withdrew, but from that moment on, South Africa became a combatant force in one of the most bitterly fought and costly civil wars in African history. As South Africa continued to deal with SWAPO on the borders of Angola, it also took the fight to the enemy, and several major conventional battles were fought between South African forces and the Soviet-backed Forcas Armadas Populares de Libertacao de Angola (FAPLA).

**The Liberation Struggle**

The imprisonment of Mandela and other key nationalists, along with the exile of many others, brought the armed struggle to an abrupt end end. Umkonto we Sizwe would continue to exist, of course, and desultory attempts were made to sustain an armed struggle, but the simple truth was that South Africa would not be defeated militarily. Its military reach and capabilities were so massively out of proportion to almost anything countering it only an unconventional war of the most asymmetric kind was ever likely to do damage.

At the time, the South African government was coming under mounting international pressure, most notably through the three major international forums of the United Nations, the British

---

[24] Thanks to the same cause and effect, the war in Rhodesia escalated rapidly after the Portuguese coup, and Red China was deeply involved in the liberation movements of Zimbabwe.

Commonwealth, and the Organization of African Unity. A popular, international anti-apartheid movement was beginning to take shape, and the focus of nationalist activity shifted into the popular arena. Both black and white South Africans assailed the arts, theater, and literature of South Africa with the anti-apartheid message. Universities in South Africa reciprocated with overseas universities, and anti-apartheid demonstrations became a regular feature of campus life.

Despite the increasing international isolation, the South African economic miracle continued, which offered an opportunity to revive a moribund black labor movement. As a result, the early 1970s were characterized not only by rising levels of protest but also by rolling industrial action.

Then, in the early 1970s, another opposition front opened up in the realm of Bantu education. In 1968, 22-year-old student Steve Biko founded the exclusively black South African Students Organization and emerged as an influential voice among black South African youth by espousing the message of "Black Consciousness," or black cultural autonomy and pride in ethnicity. As he put it, "Black consciousness is, in essence, the realization by the black man of the need to rally together with his brothers around the cause of their subjection-the blackness of their skin-and to operate as a group in order to rid themselves of the shackles that bind them to perpetual servitude." Biko also spoke of the final removal of any form of dialogue between the races. "Blacks no longer seek to reform the system, because so doing implies acceptance of the major points around which the system revolves. Blacks are out to completely transform the system and to make of it what they wish."

There was in this a strong flavor of idealism, and anyone who reads Biko's ideology of Black Consciousness cannot escape the sense that his physical survival could hardly be taken for granted. Such radical and uncompromising verbiage populated his writing that the security services and police would not take long to identify him as a target. Nonetheless, the concept of Black Consciousness struck an immediate and popular chord, achieving widespread international appeal. In June 1976, thousands of black South African schoolchildren demonstrated in Soweto, a large black township to the west of Johannesburg, protesting the requirement that lessons be taught in Afrikaans. The police opened fire, and 13-year-old student Hector Pieterson was shot and killed. The image of his body being carried by distraught friends emerged as one of the most iconic images of the anti-apartheid struggle.

Hector Pieterson would certainly not be the last. By 1977, according to the report of a detailed commission of inquiry entitled "Commission of Inquiry into the riots at Soweto and other places in South Africa held on 10 February 1977," 575 people had so far died in a similar manner, 134 of whom were under the age of 18. That same yar, Steve Biko was arrested for breaking the terms of his restriction, and a few days later he was dead. His cause of death was brain damage brought about by injuries to his head.

Steve Biko, the first high-profile martyr, very quickly became the poster child of the revolution and irrefutable evidence of the careless brutality of the regime. By then, the only African states still under white rule were Rhodesia (which was barely hanging on), South West Africa, and South Africa. The United Nations was now home to a majority of independent states, few of which hesitated to openly condemn Biko's killing and call for an end to minority rule in South Africa. In 1967, the UN created a Special Committee and a Unit on Apartheid, both organizations emitting a consistent flow of anti-apartheid messages. In 1971, the International Court of Justice handed down an opinion declaring South Africa's continued occupation of South West Africa illegal. In 1973, apartheid was declared by the UN as a crime against humanity, and in the aftermath of the Steve Biko killing, the United Nations Security Council imposed a mandatory arms embargo on South Africa. The South African arms industry, of course, was easily able to circumvent this in the short term, but the writing was definitely on the wall.

In turn, the South African government, now under the leadership of a hardliner in the form of Pieter Willem Botha, presented a picture of South Africa standing alone against the spread of communism in Africa. This was the same essential message that white Rhodesia propagated, and it was not entirely false, for the main liberation movements certainly were ideologically and materially aligned to the Communist Bloc. In this regard, South Africa was certainly confronting a hardline, communist movement in Angola, and the government tried to extrapolate from this that the ANC was a communist organization and that the communists were behind all the civil disobedience and protest in South Africa.

In truth, while the Communist Bloc and China were the only powers willingly supportive of the African liberation movement, African liberation leaders were as communist as it was necessary to be. Some, such as Julius Nyerere and Kwame Nkrumah, described themselves as "African Socialists," while Samora Machel of Mozambique and Agostino Neto of Angola frankly declared themselves Marxists. The South African Communist Party certainly formed a pillar of the domestic anti-apartheid movement, but the ANC never declared itself a communist organization, nor was its principal leadership avowedly communist. The ANC's response to the government's claim was that the black people of South Africa did not require foreign indoctrination to oppose apartheid.

One of the major difficulties in transforming passionate international opposition to apartheid into tangible economic action was the fact that South Africa was simply too important an international economic player to be shut out or shut down. South Africa was the world's major producer of gold, diamonds, and numerous other strategic minerals. A certain amount of symbolic action was taken in the aftermath of Sharpeville and on occasions of other egregious state action, but there was always a tendency to slip back into business as usual once the dust had cleared.

By 1978, however, things began to turn. As the end seemed in sight for white Rhodesia, the apartheid state in South Africa found itself increasingly against the ropes. International opposition was gathering form and direction, and the internal mechanisms established in the 1950s and 1960s to keep the whole edifice under control were beginning to fail. For this, there were numerous reasons, including white emigration, a black population explosion, the increasing demands of the military, the introduction of conscription, and the growing use of blacks in the security and military ranks. There was also the increasing cost of the Border War, and a growing difficulty of replacing aging weapons systems as the Soviet-supplied FAPLA began to overtake South Africa in state-of-the-art arms. The Bantustans remained unrecognized by any foreign power as independent states, and their continued existence was entirely thanks to South African financial support.

Then there was the fact that South Africa stood largely alone in Africa. In the Verwoerd era, Africa was governed almost entirely by European colonial governments, but by the end of the 1970s, only Rhodesia remained standing, and that was because of South African arms, balance of payment support, and fuel. In 1980, white Rhodesia finally collapsed, leaving South Africa as the last white holdout and an unmistakable anomaly on an otherwise black ruled continent.

**Reforming Apartheid**

By 1980, the popular international movement against apartheid, spearheaded by the likes of the charismatic Winnie Mandela and artists such as Hugh Masekela and Miriam Makeba, was gaining sufficient momentum to begin positively affecting international government policy. White South Africans could see where things were going, and the mood of the white population of South Africa began to tilt away from the policies of the National Party, which still entrenched in power and utterly uncompromising in its worldview, but now adrift in an unfriendly world. Even the Afrikaner movement, known for its unshakable internal cohesion, began to split as a growing movement began to advocate for some sort of a compromise.

The talk, of course, was not of a complete overhaul, but selected reforms. There remained a strong base of support for the Nats, especially in the rural and agricultural areas and in the industrial labor market, where protectionism and statutory apartheid remained the only thing separating poor whites from poor blacks. Much of the problem lay with the National Party leadership and President Botha in particular, who was by then so identified with the hardline, right-wing faction of the party that any kind of meaningful reform was impossible. He was of the virulent anti-communist faction, utterly convinced by the discredited propaganda of an earlier age and unable to see much beyond the policies already in place. His attitude to foreign pressure was to claim a communist "total onslaught," and bearing in mind the rapid descent into a police state, the security establishment was granted a disproportionate amount of influence in government. The State Security Council, created in 1972, eventually acquired more practical influence and power than the cabinet.

**Botha**

When confronted with the inevitability of reforms, the solution as Botha saw it was to somehow adapt the state to changing circumstances without yielding an iota of Afrikaans power. The changes made, therefore, were superficial at best, with only the more odious symbols of apartheid scrapped, such as signposted separate facilities. The enforcement of separation did not ease up or get eliminated anywhere, and blacks were still barred from facilities as diverse as cinemas, bars, and hotels. A commission of inquiry was authorized to consider areas of change – comprising, interestingly, of whites, Indians, and coloreds, but no blacks – and no serious consideration was given to its findings.

In 1984, a new constitution came into effect. A new Parliament was authorized, consisting of three chambers: a House of Assembly, comprising 178 white representatives elected by whites; a House of Representatives, comprising 85 coloreds voted in by coloreds; and a House of Delegates, made up of 45 Indians elected by Indians. A multiracial cabinet was drawn from all three chambers, which was responsible for what was termed "general affairs," including internal revenue, foreign affairs, defense, state security, law and order, commerce and industry, and "African affairs." Uniracial Minister's Councils assumed responsibility for their own affairs, confining their activities to areas such as education, health, and local government. The State President, replacing the prime minister, was elected by a college of 50 white, 25 colored, and 13 Indian members. The State President then appointed the members of the cabinet and the minister's councils and retained direct responsibility for dealing with issues related to blacks. Blacks were without a voice in this arrangement.

As the 1980s progressed, further cosmetic changes were made, in particular to various pass laws and group area acts, but on the whole, these were cosmetic and were ultimately intended to streamline and modify rather than abolish discriminatory statutes.

While South African leaders tried to push against the tide, the anti-apartheid movement had become a cultural touchstone across the world. Among white South Africans, much of it remained academic, and many took a defensive position against international moral grandstanding. For the average white South African, however, matters began to crystallize with the application of UN pressure on South Africa's international sports contacts. South Africa's invitation to participate in the 1964 Summer Olympics was withdrawn after a refusal by the South African sports ministry to integrate its teams. In 1976, New Zealand was censured by the International Olympic Committee for its continued sporting contacts with South Africa after a tour of South Africa by the All Blacks rugby team. South Africa's final foreign rugby tour was to New Zealand in 1981, and although some rogue British and French teams toured South Africa amid much international disapprobation, the nail in the coffin of South African rugby came with the exclusion of the Springboks for the 1987 and 1991 World Cup tournaments.

Also throughout the 1980s, domestic protests continued, featuring school boycotts, bus boycotts, worker stay-aways, and regular clashes between residents of the townships and police. Inter-black violence also became a feature of township life as political resistance overlapped into gang violence and rival groups adopted political language and opposing political associations.

In 1985, Winnie Mandela, the wife of jailed nationalist Nelson Mandela, defied a banning order that restricted her to the town of Brandfort in the Orange Free State by appearing in the Johannesburg township of Soweto. The mass movement in Johannesburg and other major South African cities tended by be organized and orchestrated by the South African Congress of Trade Unions, or COSATU, and the various liberation parties. Winnie Mandela, however, always militant and uncompromising, introduced a far more aggressive tone to the business of anti-apartheid activism. As an international figure, she attracted an enormous popular following, and she was almost single-handedly responsible for popularizing the anti-apartheid message and keeping Mandela's name at the forefront of the international debate. She was deeply stigmatized in South Africa for her support and advocacy of the excruciatingly violent methods in common use in the townships.

**Nelson and Winnie Mandela**

On April 13, 1985, dressed in combat fatigues, Winnie Mandela delivered a speech in Munsieville Johannesburg, during which she uttered the now infamous slogan, "Together, hand-in-hand with our sticks of matches, with our necklaces, we shall liberate this country." The reference here was to the grisly practice of "necklacing," a style of street punishment that involved hanging a vehicle tire around the neck of a victim, filling it with gasoline, and igniting it. This apparent endorsement of the darker side of the anti-apartheid movement earned Winnie Mandela a great deal of informal censure, and the South African government was gifted with the opportunity to cite her as an example of what might be expected under African rule. The precedents elsewhere in Africa were already unimpressive, and at about that time, the term "Afro-pessimism" began to be coined in the international press as a lamentation on the apparent inability of Africa to effectively govern itself.

Winnie Mandela's violent manifestation of anti-apartheid protest continued with the activities of the "Nelson Mandela Football Club," the enforcement arm of the Winnie Mandela personality cult, which was responsible for numerous abductions, beatings, and killings. There were many other similar gangs and mobs active throughout South Africa, and the government was frequently guilty of fermenting this violence through covert funding and assistance.

Thus, by the end of the decade, the situation in the townships began to resemble a formal insurrection. As scenes of South African violence were splashed across television screens, the image of armored troop carriers and heavily armed convoys of police patrolling the townships became a nightly feature. Meanwhile, the demographic weight of the white population in South Africa began to steadily diminish as the black population grew at an unequal pace and as the best and brightest of whites began to flee the country in search of better prospects elsewhere. In markets where South African goods were not boycotted, they were non-competitive, and a spate of sanctions and divestments began to deeply impact the health of the economy.

Perhaps most importantly, the myth of a self-sufficient peasantry in the Bantustans was visible, as was the equally flawed myth of white separation. Blacks needed urban employment (the Bantustans were supported by remittances), and urban industry needed black labor. The very foundation of separation was untenable and held together only by the ideological resistance and determination of an oppressive government. By the 1990s, substantial numbers of blacks were educated, and a strong and vociferous black middle class was emerging. Institutionalized, government-sponsored efforts to continue their marginalization no longer made any practical sense.

## The End of Apartheid

As the institution of apartheid hung in the balance, the Berlin Wall fell, and the Soviet Union began its rapid collapse. The notion that South Africa was suffering a "total onslaught" by the forces of communism was obviously undermined by the end of the Cold War. While this marked the end of several African regimes that were only being kept alive by Cold War patronage, it also set in motion events that would result in the end of apartheid rule in South Africa.

On the battlefields in northern South West Africa and Angola, things were shaken up. As the Cold War dynamic, that which had added so much fuel to so many African wars, began to fade away, Angolan oil reserves quickly replaced Soviet funding as the driving factor of war. Moreover, as South Africa's influence inevitably waned, the war simply continued to be fought on revised terms until 2002 when National Union for the Total Independence of Angola leader Jonas Savimbi was killed.

In December 1988, Cuba and the Soviet Union agreed to link their withdrawal from Angola to South Africa's withdrawal from South West Africa. This was a face-saving formula for the two sides to end a war that had achieved almost nothing. The opening months of 1989 saw the beginning of a massive operation to return to South Africa a military operation that had been present in Ovamboland for upward of 23 years. At the same time, the first units of the "United Nations Transition Assistance Group" (UNTAG) began to arrive in South West Africa, forming an interim authority as a prelude to full Namibian independence, which was celebrated on March 21, 1990.

As the SADF withdrew from Namibia, it did so against the backdrop of a general mood of change. It was becoming clear to all that the government could not support the institutions of apartheid indefinitely, but the liberation movement and the international community also had to acknowledge that the government of South Africa could not be forcibly overthrown. Moreover, the longer the stalemate continued, the greater the residual damage to both sides.

As early as 1985, tentative, non-governmental contacts were underway between the leadership of the ANC in exile and prominent white business leaders and liberal civic leaders and politicians. There were also somewhat less formal contacts between prominent individuals on both sides. Even the hard-right Afrikaner Resistance Movement (AWB) began to air the notion of an independent Afrikaner homeland in South Africa, which was clear a sign of impending change as any other to date.

Meanwhile, as the government of P.W. Botha continued trying to manage the situation with force, behind the scenes, covert government contacts were underway with none other than Nelson Mandela. While he had been incarcerated for over a quarter of a century, Mandela's name had never disappeared from the popular movement, and by the end of the 1980s, largely through the efforts of his wife, his was the name around which the liberation movement rallied.

Initially, the gist of these contacts was to try and sell Mandela on the idea of his own freedom in exchange for abstention from politics, which inevitably proved to be a waste of time. He was moved from Robbin Island to a more commodious accommodation at Pollsmoor Prison outside Cape Town. There, believing that a solution could be negotiated, he began a series of meetings with South African officials. By 1988, demands that he renounce the armed struggle, the alliance of the ANC, and the South African Communist Party had also proved fruitless, and as the weeks and months were ticking by, it became clear that Mandela, notwithstanding his incarceration, held all of the cards. He was moved to a house located in the grounds of the Victor Verster Prison in Paarl, where he was treated as a guest and allowed unlimited and unsupervised visits, which meant he was essentially given the freedom to organize. A 10-page memorandum was compiled under his signature and sent to the office of President PW Both, stating, "I now consider it necessary in the national interest for the African National Congress and the government to meet urgently to negotiate an effective political settlement."

Mandela added to this the point that the armed struggle was simply a reflection of the violence perpetrated against the masses by the government and that the ANC's alliance with the communist party was simply an expedient of the Freedom Struggle. If the basis of the Struggle was removed, it would disappear, along with the communist alliance. Cautiously, the ANC leadership in exile endorsed this position, announcing, in what was known as the Harare Declaration, that a negotiated end to apartheid was possible.

In January 1989, almost on cue, President Botha suffered a stroke and resigned as National Party leader. By choice of a parliamentary caucus, the presidency passed to the 53-year-old Frederik Willem de Klerk. De Klerk was no less a product of Afrikaner nationalism than Botha, but his relative youth and pragmatism better positioned him to act on a sense of inevitability that had by then permeated throughout white society. On February 2, 1990, he made the momentous announcement that bans on the ANC, the Communist Party, and the PAC were to be lifted. Political prisoners incarcerated for nonviolent actions were released, and some 33 domestic organizations were legalized. Nine days later, Nelson Mandela was unconditionally released after 27 years behind bars.

**De Klerk**

For the first time since its banning in 1961, the ANC held its annual conference in South Africa, and in a difficult and at times rancorous process involving some 2,244 delegates, a banned and secret organization began its transition to a mass following political party with a practical, democratic political agenda. Oliver Tambo, leader of the ANC through the difficult years, did not stand for reelection, as it was obvious there could be no other candidate than Mandela. A 66 member national executive committee was also elected, and at the head of the party, Mandela began to apply his mind to the negotiation of a fresh constitution within which the hopes of the nation resided.

Shortly after Mandela's release in February 1990, he set about traveling to seek affinities in prestigious circles in Sweden and Britain, and he put in an appearance at the Nelson Mandela: American International Tribute for a Free South Africa concert. None of this was done without purpose, and where Mandela might have once toured solely to seek help, he was now projecting the strength of international solidarity in preparation for some diplomatic muscle-flexing with the new president. Whatever steel curtain Mandela had experienced with Botha, an entirely new set of difficulties was presented by de Klerk, who wrestled with ongoing feelings of humiliation at the hands of the upstart African leader. Fully aware that Mandela had toured Africa, Scandinavia and Britain, and that he had been welcomed by Pope John Paul II, Margaret Thatcher, George H.W, Bush, Venkataraman of India, Suharto of Indonesia, Mahathir Mohammad of Malaysia and Australia's Bob Hawke, de Klerk's awareness of the international support behind Mandela in their first meetings was likely felt all the more keenly.

In 1990, Mandela led a delegation to negotiate with 11 Afrikaner men from the South African government, and this in itself demonstrated de Klerk's undermined confidence and a general realization that the old order would no longer stand. This effort led to the Grot Schuur Minute, in which the government lifted the state of emergency, though the ANC's reciprocal offer of a ceasefire was not born entirely out of humanitarian motivations but in part because of a recognized disadvantage in firepower.

Mandela was elected President of the ANC in 1991 at the National Conference, and he acquired an office in the new ANC headquarters in Johannesburg. Many on both sides were caught off-guard by Mandela's sense of moderation in his dealings with his own people and the opposition, including his own wife; Winnie, ever less patient and more prepared to strike boldly, became thoroughly disenchanted with this careful, methodical style of revolution. Her involvement in the larger picture would be, for a time, rendered moot after being convicted of kidnapping and assault and sentenced to six years in prison by the Truth and Reconciliation Commission. Despite her post-apartheid internal status as "mother of the nation," her presence during the transitional process was less welcome among moderate factions. Furthermore, after she was accused of gross mismanagement of funds, a lightly-veiled criminal indictment, she was forced from the National Executive.

Mandela and de Klerk were natural antagonists, and bad blood prevailed throughout negotiations in which de Klerk labored under a persistent belief that Mandela was attempting to belittle him at every turn. He also lived with the particular onus of being the white South African President who would let the old dream die. In addition to de Klerk foreseeing apartheid's eventual undoing, and fearing taking the blame for it, an integrated society with shared power of majority rule was the most offensive and unworkable idea to him of all. He made his disdain for the process clear in the wasted efforts of December 1991 during the Convention for a Democratic South Africa (CODESA 1). President de Klerk used his time not to build common ground but to condemn ANC violence, and an equally offended Mandela took the microphone to denounce the basis of de Klerk's legitimacy to exist as a minority ruler at all. In the 1992 session, de Klerk maintained his insistence that any post-apartheid South Africa must be federalized, and Mandela naturally objected to this, demanding that the post-apartheid period must be overseen by a unitary government of majority rule. An alarming rate of violence between black factions similarly threatened the process, and terrorist-incursions by the Inkatha faction worked against Mandela's hope to maintain a tepid emotional temperature to ensure minimal reprisals in the post-apartheid period. Thousands died in these actions, and Mandela personally faulted de Klerk for overly demonstrative retaliations, such as in what was termed the Sebokeng Massacre, where over 18,000 homes that had been erected by the government gave way to violent clashes over rent and service tariff boycotts. A peace accord was signed, but gang violence remained a regular feature of the area.

After more massacres at Boipatong and Bisho, Mandela called for international peacekeepers, and given the ongoing public opinion internationally, the subservient faction pleading for outside help played much better in the press than Inkatha murders of 40 citizens or the killing of 28 by the Ciskei Defense Force. The United Nations sent Cyrus Vance to participate in the negotiations following Mandela's call for the convening of a Security Council session; Mandela's request was perceived as a triumph of nobility over oppression in much of the outer world.

As this delicate state of affairs progressed, threats to the peace still loomed from militant organizations like the Concerned South Africans Group, a coalition of rightist Afrikaner parties and black secessionists. Terrorist attacks continued from both fringes, with Inkatha actions from the left and white supremacists from the right, such as the Afrikaner Weerstandbeweging, who attacked the Kempton World Trade Center in the summer of 1993. The ANC leader, Chris Hani, was murdered in that year, and the peace process grew more vulnerable with each violent news item.

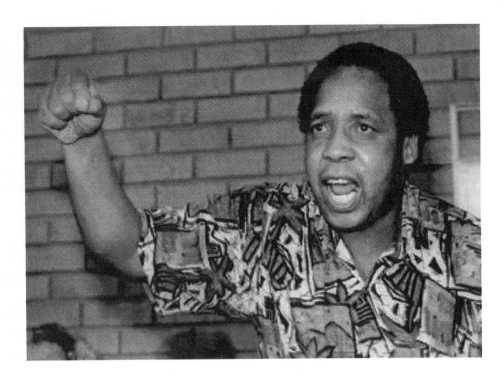

**Hani**

Realizing that the situation was worsening, Mandela returned to negotiations with added fervor, demanding that all traditional Zulu weapons be banned and that Zulu hostels be fenced off, to which de Klerk, in a rare spirit of cooperation, agreed. In the end, both sides consented to a five-year coalition government underpinned by an American-inspired Bill of Rights. The ANC somewhat reluctantly agreed to protect all white civil service jobs, which was essential to Mandela's bloodless transition, because if the white-based economy was destroyed, the new South Africa, already crippled economically, would collapse and start again with nothing. The country was divided into nine provinces, each with its own civic structure, and each represented by its own localized premier.

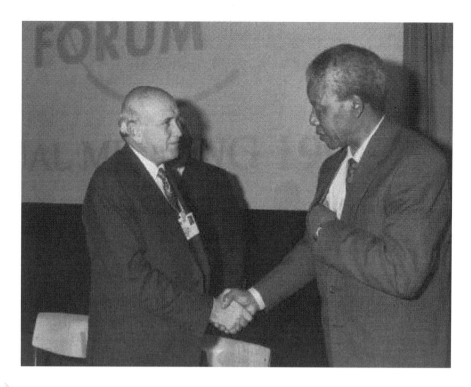

**Mandela and de Klerk shake hands at the World Economic Forum, 1992**

In July, Mandela and de Klerk each received the Liberty Medal from President Bill Clinton, but the fact that the awards were bestowed on separate trips is more than telling. Not long after, they were jointly awarded the Nobel Peace Prize, and in his acceptance speech, Mandela called for continuing the fight against apartheid:

> "Together, we join two distinguished South Africans, the late Chief Albert Lutuli and His Grace Archbishop Desmond Tutu, to whose seminal contributions to the peaceful struggle against the evil system of apartheid you paid well-deserved tribute by awarding them the Nobel Peace Prize. It will not be presumptuous of us if we also add, among our predecessors, the name of another outstanding Nobel Peace Prize winner, the late Rev Martin Luther King Jr. He, too, grappled with and died in the effort to make a contribution to the just solution of the same great issues of the day which we have had to face as South Africans. We speak here of the challenge of the dichotomies of war and peace, violence and non-violence, racism and human dignity, oppression and repression and liberty and human rights, poverty and freedom from want.

> "We stand here today as nothing more than a representative of the millions of our people who dared to rise up against a social system whose very essence is war, violence, racism, oppression, repression and the impoverishment of an entire people.

"I am also here today as a representative of the millions of people across the globe, the anti-apartheid movement, the governments and organizations that joined with us, not to fight against South Africa as a country or any of its peoples, but to oppose an inhuman system and sue for a speedy end to the apartheid crime against humanity.

"These countless human beings, both inside and outside our country, had the nobility of spirit to stand in the path of tyranny and injustice, without seeking selfish gain. They recognized that an injury to one is an injury to all and therefore acted together in defense of justice and a common human decency.

"Because of their courage and persistence for many years, we can, today, even set the dates when all humanity will join together to celebrate one of the outstanding human victories of our century.

"When that moment comes, we shall, together, rejoice in a common victory over racism, apartheid and white minority rule."

However, the mutual chasm would continue between the two until the end of negotiations and well into the new state. Mandela, acutely aware of South Africa's tenuous financial condition, which would grow far worse if the revolution spilled over into sectarian violence or outright civil war, began to seek out foreign investors of every political and economic persuasion, even as he experienced no small amount of trouble in moderating his sense of nationalism. At the root of it, Mandela would have preferred for the black population to create the new wealth as he did for them to create the revolution single-handedly, but neither was possible.

Despite never having been perceived as a great orator, by the time 1994's general election came around, Mandela's supporters had established a vast network of forums around the country at which Mandela would speak. Despite his verbal limitations, Mandela was intensely popular, and to many, simply seeing him and meeting him was better than hearing him speak. During the campaign, Mandela and de Klerk debated on live television, and although there was little chance of overcoming the president's rhetorical mastery, Mandela shocked the viewership by offering his hand at the onset in a gesture of cooperation, which was perceived as a victory in itself.

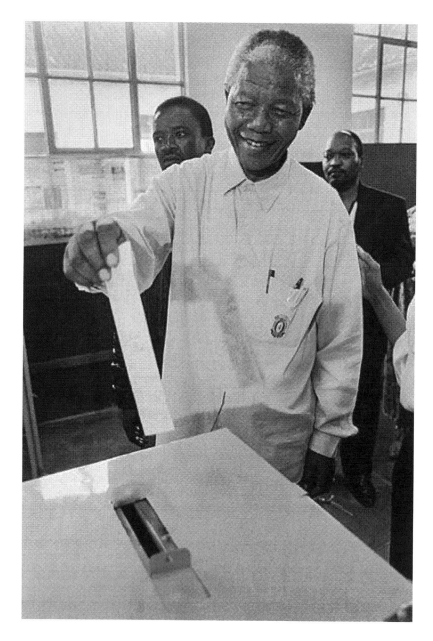

**Mandela casting his vote in the 1994 election**

Ultimately, the ANC and its first African candidate took 62% of the national vote in the general election of 1994, a victory to be sure but a disappointment as well, because the figure fell just short of the two-thirds majority needed to alter the constitution without challenges. The Inkatha and National parties each took one of the nine provinces, but Nelson Mandela, the first African President of the Republic of South Africa, was inaugurated on May 10, 1994, an event televised around the world. In his inauguration speech, Mandela declared:

> "Democracy is based on the majority principle. This is especially true in a country such as ours where the vast majority have been systematically denied their rights. At the same time, democracy also requires that the rights of political and other

minorities be safeguarded.

"In the political order we have established there will regular, open and free elections, at all levels of government — central, provincial and municipal. There shall also be a social order which respects completely the culture, language and religious rights of all sections of our society and the fundamental rights of the individual.

"The task at hand on will not be easy. But you have mandated us to change South Africa from a country in which the majority lived with little hope, to one in which they can live and work with dignity, with a sense of self-esteem and confidence in the future. The cornerstone of building a better life of opportunity, freedom and prosperity is the Reconstruction and Development Programme.

"This needs unity of purpose. It needs in action. It requires us all to work together to bring an end to division, an end to suspicion and build a nation united in our diversity."

A daily newspaper editor in Johannesburg, remarking on Mandela's ability to equalize the "haves" and "have nots," rather than giving one over to the other for bloodletting, wrote, "The way the election was conducted – all its imperfections notwithstanding – is proof that this country has just survived a negotiated revolution." Analyzing the concept of a negotiated revolution, Nina Koshey went on to say that "to Nelson Mandela the election was liberation, and to Justice Kiegler, the chief of the independent election commission, it was an act of national reconciliation." Mandela had successfully engineered a government of national unity that was dominated by the African National Congress, and de Klerk became the Deputy President.

**President Clinton and President Mandela**

Led by Mandela, who was 76 when he took power in South Africa, the overthrow of apartheid had finally been realized.

**Online Resources**

Other titles about South Africa on Amazon

**Bibliography**

Berger, Carl (1970). The Sense of Power; Studies in the Ideas of Canadian Imperialism,: 1867–1914. University of Toronto Press. pp. 233–34. ISBN 978-0-8020-6113-3.

Bester, R. (1994). Boer Rifles and Carbines of the Anglo-Boer Warb. Bloemfontein: War Museum of the Boer Republics.

Blake, Albert (2010). Boereverraaier. Tafelberg. p. 46.

"Case Name: Anglo-Boer: Britain's Vietnam (1899–1902)". American University of Washington D.C Trade Environment projects. Retrieved 21 July 2016.

Desai, Ashwin; Vahed, Goolem (2015). The South African Gandhi: Stretcher-bearer of Empire. Stanford University Press.

"Miscellaneous information: Cost of the war". AngloBoerWar.com. 2015. Retrieved 12 September 2015.[unreliable source?]

Chase, Sean (4 November 2012). "Dragoons remember the heroes of Leliefontein". Daily Observer.

Daily Mail (5810). 16 November 1914. pp. 4 ff. ISSN 0307-7578. Missing or empty |title= (help)

Duffy, Michael (22 August 2009). "Sam Hughes Biography". firstworldwar.com.[unreliable source?]

Cameron, Trewhella, ed. (1986). An Illustrated History of South Africa. Johannesburg,: Jonathan Ball. p. 207.

Cartwright, A. P (1964). The Dynamite Company. Cape Town: Purnell & Sons.

Davis, Richard Harding (1900). With Both Armies In South Africa. Charles Scribner Sons. p. 34, fn. 59.

"South African War (British-South African history)". Encyclopedia Britannica. Britannica.com. 31 March 2011. Retrieved 23 July 2013.

"Caring for the soldiers health". Nash's war manual. London: Eveleigh Nash. 1914. p. 309.

Farwell, Byron (March 1976). "Taking Sides in the Boer War". American Heritage Magazine. 20 (3). ISSN 0002-8738. Archived from the original on 7 January 2009.

Ferguson, Niall (2002). Empire: The Rise and Demise of the British World Order and the Lessons for Global Power. Basic Books. p. 235.

Grundlingh, Albert (1980). "Collaborators in Boer Society". In Warwick, P. The South African War. London. pp. 258–78.

Granatstein, J.L. (2010). The Oxford Companion to Canadian Military History. Oxford University Press. ISBN 978-0-19-543088-2.

Grattan, Robert (2009). "The Entente in World War I: a case study in strategy formulation in an alliance". Journal of Management History. 15 (2): 147–58.

Gronum, M.A. (1977). Die ontplooiing van die Engelse Oorlog 1899–1900. Tafelberg.

Haydon, A.P. (1964). "South Australia's first war". Australian Historical Studies. 11 (42).

Hayes, Matthew Horace (1902). Horses on board ship: a guide to their management. London: Hurst and Blackett. pp. 213–14.

Jeffery, Keith (2000). "The Irish Soldier in the Boer War". In Gooch, John. The Boer War. London: Cass. p. 145. cites

Inglis, Brian (1974). Roger Casement. London: Coronet Books. pp. 53–55.

Jacson, M. (1908). "II". The Record of a Regiment of the Line. Hutchinson & Company. p. 88. ISBN 1-4264-9111-5.

Jones, Maurig (1996). "Blockhouses of the Boer War". Colonial Conquest, magweb. Archived from the original on 13 May 2008. Retrieved 10 May 2008.

Jones, Huw M. (October 1999). Neutrality compromised: Swaziland and the Anglo-Boer War, 1899–1902. Military History Journal. 11.

Judd, Denis; Surridge, Keith (2013). The Boer War: A History (2nd ed.). London: I. B. Tauris. ISBN 978-1780765914.excerpt and text search; a standard scholarly history

Keppel-Jones, Arthur (1983). Rhodes and Rhodesia: The White Conquest of Zimbabwe, 1884–1902. Montreal, Quebec and Kingston, Ontario: McGill-Queen's University Press. pp. 590–99. ISBN 978-0-7735-0534-6.

McElwee, William (1974). The Art of War: Waterloo to Mons. London: Purnell. pp. 223–29. ISBN 0-253-31075-X.

"Relative Value of UK£: using Economic Power in 2014 (using the share of GDP)". Five Ways to Compute the Relative Value of a UK Pound Amount, 1270 to Present. Measuringworth.com. 2015. Retrieved 12 September 2015.

Marsh, Peter T. (1994). Joseph Chamberlain: Entrepreneur in Politics. Yale University Press. pp. 482–522.

Meintjes, Johannes (1974). President Paul Kruger: A Biography (First ed.). London: Cassell. ISBN 978-0-304-29423-7.

Morris, Michael; Linnegar, John (2004). Every Step of the Way: The Journey to Freedom in South Africa. Ministry of Education. pp. 58–95. ISBN 0-7969-2061-3.

Nathan, M. (1941). Paul Kruger: His Life And Times. Durban: Knox.

O'Brien, P. (1988). The Costs and Benefits of British Imperialism 1846–1914. Past & Present.

O'Leary, Michael (29 December 1999). "Regimental Rouge – Battles of the Boer War". Regimental Rouge.

Pakenham, Thomas (1979). The Boer War. New York: Random House. ISBN 0-394-42742-4.

Peddie, John (22 August 2009). "John McCrae Biography". firstworldwar.com.

Pocock, Roger S. (1917). Horses. London: J. Murray. p. viii fn. 11. ISBN 0-665-99382-X.

Powell, Sean-Andre (2015). How Did Winston S. Churchill's Experience As A Prisoner Of War: During The Boer War Affect His Leadership Style And Career?. Pickle Partners Publishing.

Onselen, Charles van (1982). "Chapter 1:New Babylon". Studies in the Social and Economic History of the Witwatersrand, 1886–1914. London: Longman. ISBN 9780582643840.

Onselen, Charles van (October 2003). "'The Modernization of the Zuid Afrikaansche Republiek: F. E. T. Krause, J. C. Smuts, and the Struggle for the Johannesburg Public Prosecutor's Office, 1898–1899". Law and History Review. American Society for Legal History. 21 (3): 483–526. doi:10.2307/3595118.

Pakenham, Thomas (1991) [1979]. The Boer War. London: Cardinal. p. 571. ISBN 0-7474-0976-5.

Pakenham, Thomas (1991a). The Scramble for Africa. p. 573. ISBN 0-380-71999-1.

Ploeger, Jan (1985). "Burgers in Britse Diens (1902)". Scientia Militaria. 15 (1): 15–22.

Pretorius, Fransjohan (2000). "The Experience of the Bitter-Ender Boer". In Gooch, John. The Boer War: Direction, Experience and Image. London: Cass. p. 179.

Pretorius, Fransjohan (2011). "Anglo-Boer war". In Jacobs, S.; Johnson, K. Encyclopedia of South Africa.

Pulsifer, Cameron (2017). "For Queen and Country: Canadians and the South African War". Canadian War Museum. Retrieved 2 February 2017.

"The South African War 1899–1902". South African History Online. 10 November 2011. Retrieved 29 January 2017.

Searle, G.R. (2004). A new England?: peace and war, 1886–1918. Oxford University Press. pp. 269–307.

Spies, S.B. (1977). Methods of Barbarism: Roberts and Kitchener and Civilians in the Boer Republics January 1900 – May 1902. Cape Town: Human & Rousseau. p. 265.

Steele, David (2000). "Salisbury and the Soldiers". In Gooch, John. The Boer War: Direction, Experience and Image. London: Cass.

Stirling, John (17 February 2009). "Gordon Highlanders (extract)". Our Regiments in South Africa. Naval and Military Press.

Surridge, Keith (2000). "Lansdowne at the War Office". In Gooch, John. The Boer War: Direction, Experience and Image. London: Cass. p. 24.

Swardt, Eric (1998). "The JJ Potgieter Manuscript" (PDF). p. 97. Retrieved 23 August 2009.

Villiers, J.C. de (June 1984). "The Medical Aspect of the Anglo-Boer War, 1899–1902 Part ll". Military History Journal. 6 (3):[page needed].

Warwick, Peter (1983). Black People and the South African War, 1899–1902. Cambridge University Press.

Watt, S (December 1982). "Intombi Military Hospital and Cemetery". Military History Journal. Die Suid-Afrikaanse Krygshistoriese Vereniging. 5 (6).

Webb, Peter (2010). "The Silent Flag in the New Fallen Snow: Sara Jeannette Duncan and the Legacy of the South African War". Journal of Canadian Studies. University of Toronto Press. 44 (1): 75–90.

Wessels, André (2000). "Afrikaners at War". In Gooch, John. The Boer War: Direction, Experience and Image. London: Cass.

Wessels, André (2010). A Century of Postgraduate Anglo-Boer War (1899–1902) Studies: Masters' and Doctoral Studies Completed at Universities in South Africa, in English-speaking Countries and on the European Continent, 1908–2008. African Sun Media. p. 32. ISBN 978-1-920383-09-1.

Wessels, André (2011). The Anglo-Boer War 1889–1902: White Man's War, Black Man's War, Traumatic War. African Sun Media. p. 79. ISBN 978-1-920383-27-5.

Wessels, Elria (2009). "Boers positions in the Klipriviersberg". Veldslae-Anglo-Boereoorlog 1899–1902. Archived from the original on 14 February 2013.

Witton, George (2003). Scapegoats of the Empire: The True Story of Breaker Morant's Bushveldt Carbineers.[full citation needed]

Yap, Melanie; Leong Man, Dainne (1996). Colour, Confusion and Concessions: The History of the Chinese in South Africa. Hong Kong: Hong Kong University Press. p. 510. ISBN 962-209-423-6.

## Free Books by Charles River Editors

We have brand new titles available for free most days of the week. To see which of our titles are currently free, click on this link.

## Discounted Books by Charles River Editors

We have titles at a discount price of just 99 cents everyday. To see which of our titles are currently 99 cents, click on this link.

Made in the USA
Columbia, SC
02 June 2024

36539020R00085